Book Description

Are you considering taking up the boondocking lifestyle? Whether boondocking on a permanent or part-time basis, you are going to need a bit of guidance. There are facets of this way of life that have a lot more reasoning and meaning to them than what you see on the surface.

Not all RVing is boondocking and yet all boondocking requires an RV. What is boondocking? The first thing you need to know is that RVing at its very best is not parking at a campsite. In fact, all those convenient connections to the spigots and electrical receptacles make it the very opposite of boondocking.

In all honesty, you must already have some idea of what the real thing is about. Perhaps you have thought of taking your RV into the sticks already, but you have not arrived at the decision yet. Maybe it is the things you have heard of and the questions that are unanswered. If that is the case, then this is just the book for you.

"Off-Grid RV—A Technical Guide to Self-Sufficient Boondocking" is a book that covers every aspect of boondocking. Where needed, it gets technical, and it focuses on etiquette and good practices of the lifestyle without forgetting the environment.

Off-Grid RV--A Technical Guide to Self-Sufficient Boondocking

Learn the Know-How, and Redefine How to Boondock in Modern Ways

By Lee Martin

© Copyright 2021 - All rights reserved.

The content contained within this book may not be reproduced, duplicated or transmitted without direct written permission from the author or the publisher.

Under no circumstances will any blame or legal responsibility be held against the publisher, or author, for any damages, reparation, or monetary loss due to the information contained within this book, either directly or indirectly.

Legal Notice:

This book is copyright protected. It is only for personal use. You cannot amend, distribute, sell, use, quote or paraphrase any part, or the content within this book, without the consent of the author or publisher.

Disclaimer Notice:

Please note the information contained within this document is for educational and entertainment purposes only. All effort has been executed to present accurate, up to date, reliable, complete information. No warranties of any kind are declared or implied. Readers acknowledge that the author is not engaged in the rendering of legal, financial, medical or professional advice. The content within this book has been derived from various sources. Please consult a licensed professional before attempting any techniques outlined in this book.

By reading this document, the reader agrees that under no circumstances is the author responsible for any losses, direct or indirect, that are incurred as a result of the use of the information contained within this document, including, but not limited to, errors, omissions, or inaccuracies.

Table of Contents

Part 1 1
How to Boondock 1

Chapter 1 2
What Is Boondocking? 2
Chapter 2 7
Preparing for the Journey 7
Chapter 3 14
Urban and City Docking 14
Chapter 4 22
The Right Vehicle for the Job 22
Chapter 5 28
Safety First 28
Chapter 6 37
Minimize Your Footprint 37
Chapter 7 44
The List of Everything You Will Need for Boondocking 44
Chapter 8 56
Is America Boondock Friendly? 56

Part 2 70
Powering Your RV 70

Chapter 1 71
Minimum Electrical Requirements 71

Chapter 2 77
Understanding Your Electrical System 77

Chapter 3 84
Inverters 84

Chapter 4 94
Generators 94

Chapter 5 102
Amp Hours 102

Chapter 6 109
Transfer Switches 109

Chapter 7 113
Batteries 113

Chapter 8 120
Solar Power 120

Part 3 128

Optimizing Your RV 128

Chapter 1 129
Types of RVs and Their Functions 129

Chapter 2 135
Accessories 135

Chapter 3 142
Water, Waste Management, and Temperature Control . 142

Chapter 4 149
Boondocking; Fallacies, Truths, and Etiquette 149

Chapter 5 156
Turning Your RV Into a Workspace 156

Chapter 6	162
Full-Time RVing	162
Chapter 7	165
Boondocking Abroad	165
Conclusion	169
References	171

Introduction

The original version of the word 'boondock' means 'mountain,' but when used colloquially, it is indicative of isolated areas away from civilization. Common stigma suggests that people who hail from these places are unsophisticated and primitive in behavior and thinking. The irony is that the word is not even of American origins. It hails from the Filipino word 'bundók,' which is of the Tagalog dialect (dictionary.com, 2020).

The word arrived on American shores with soldiers returning from the war in the Philippines around 1890 (Merriam-Webster, n.d.-b).

To this day, it is still used with humorous connotations.

In the American outdoor culture, boondocking does not even refer to a rural area anymore, as these areas still have some kind of community. While it may indicate the environmental setting of an isolated campsite, RVing in this setting is still not boondocking.

You are boondocking when in the furthest place from a city, town, or any center of civilization. You are there with your RV because areas like those have no access to public utilities and thus you will be off the grid, and guess what, people go there for fun.

Being off the grid takes skill, knowledge, and the correct way of thinking. The latter is generally synonymous with living out in the sticks and can be quite a challenge. Everything is limited, and whatever resources you have are not as easily accessed as when you are in the city.

What Is Off-Grid?

There are different versions of being off-grid, but the generally accepted meaning of the term is when you are independent of public utilities. These utilities include, but are not limited to, electricity, sewage systems, water services, and piped gas. People who choose to live off the grid commit on different levels, with some going the whole nine yards and others finding a middle ground, which means they opt to be partially dependent on public utilities. Living off the grid is possible for homes of different sizes and designs. One version of an off-grid home is a recreational vehicle (RV).

Off-the-grid (OTG) living speaks of independence and a higher level of self-sufficiency. OTG is not necessarily cutting out the use of electricity, gas, or water, but rather creating your own reserves as opposed to using from a centralized source. OTG is an outstanding feature of boondocking.

Thanks to technology, detaching from the grid does not mean that you have to go back in time. For the right price, you can enjoy all the pleasures of your home, far from the confines of suburbia. This convenience is made possible by the RV.

Being a combination of a home and vehicle, the RV allows you the best of both worlds, and thanks to ongoing innovation, the level of mobility and comfort is constantly improving. The advantage of not being location-bound is that you get to see more, and unlike other forms of off-gridding, you do not need to commit to one environment.

General Motivations

People enjoy the boondocking concept as a lifestyle for different reasons, but for many, the main motivation for OTG living is breaking away from society. When making this change the off-gridder will usually go to a location without public utilities. As such, disconnection from the grid will follow naturally. The most an off-gridder can commit to depends on sustaining food sources like crops and livestock. The level of investment in such a scenario is indicative of the lifestyle at its most permanent.

There are no available statistics for the number of Americans living this way, but it is a developing trend. A striking characteristic of such a lifestyle is that it is cheaper and, in most cases, healthier. These benefits extend to boondocking, too, which is the same thing but as a form of leisure.

There is an eco-friendly aspect to such a lifestyle. As noted, being self-sufficient comes with limited resources, and as such you are obligated to consume conservatively. Resources in this context refer to your water supply, the limited wastewater capacity, and power reserves. Provided that you adhere to environmentally friendly practices, not only will you engage in a pastime that is healthy and fun but also one that is eco-friendly.

Part 1

How to Boondock

Chapter 1

What Is Boondocking?

What defines this ever-growing form of recreation?

Boondocking, to put it simply, is the practice of spending a night or more at a location that is isolated, outlying, and off the grid. The RV, irrespective of shape and size, is an essential accessory to the activity.

The Origins of the Practice

It is difficult to put a finger on the advent of boondocking. This is likely because every generation before the 1700s found themselves in the boonies. On the other hand, before there were the power services and piped water connections there was nothing but the outback.

The boom towns and the railway camps of the late 1800s consisted mainly of tents. These tent cities had no hookups, and the closest thing to dry camping back then was cold camping without any fire. Dry camping, as it is known today, only came with the advent of electricity. The tent colonies of that era, even though in the middle of nature, cannot be considered as a form of boondocking. The fur trapper with his packhorse in the mountains far from any town was a better representation of a boondocker, and this was due to his isolation from society.

The aforementioned lifestyle during America's early years was a necessity for many, but western storytellers speak of a lonesome breed of men and their love for the wilderness. These men sought out the hidden valleys and canyons well after it was no longer crucial to their survival. Humanity's love for nature, it seems, has been around for a while.

Today, despite the megalopolises, interstate highways, airports, and railways, there are still far-flung outback areas. As suburbia encroached on nature, and the cities grew, so did the desire to escape these concrete jungles, even if only temporarily.

Today, an outdoor culture prevails. It is in a constant state of growth becoming more distinct and forever the alternative to the bright city lights.

Living a fulfilling life in such a natural setting is often seen as a luxury. While there are many outdoor hobbyists, and the industries that serve their needs are well-developed, most people can only enjoy the outdoors in little doses. The latter is not so much because it is expensive but rather because of their obligations and livelihoods that bind them to the city.

There are many industries dedicated to serving the great outdoors. These range from the state-run forestry services and national parks to the service providers like guides and the manufacturers of tents and other outdoor essentials. Finally, there are those responsible for the production of high-ticket items like RVs.

What Makes It Boondocking?

Boondocking is unique and there are a few salient characteristics that define it. Though it may be generalized as camping (along with other forms of outdoor living), it is unlike camping in so many ways.

With all the options available to the aspiring outdoorsman, the RV has become the most effective tool. It allows you to go farther away from humanity and civilization and provides the highest level of independence through well-developed functionalities. Additionally, this mode of outdoor recreation provides a relatively high degree of comfort.

The RV allows you to fulfill every aspect and criteria of boondocking. Without it, your capabilities are hampered, and thus it is just not the same.

The Usual Comforts

Your home in suburbia has fully equipped living spaces with everything that makes you comfortable. Things like mobile networks and a store just down the road along with other amenities are inherent features of the average residential area. The neighbor on each side of you (convenient for when you run out of sugar) and the postman dropping the mail are typical features of your normal life.

Every boondocker will miss at least one of the latter at some point. Be that as it may, outdoor culture has advanced to the point that you can have almost all the comforts of the home contained and mobilized. The things that can not be substituted are what define the experience and the reasons you do it in the first place.

A certain school of thought may suggest that one goes boondocking to get away from these comforts and interact with nature. Well, the decision is yours to make. Will you drive a hundred miles from society and still want to watch the Super Bowl? With the technology available today, it is possible.

Dry Camping

Is dry camping boondocking? Driving your tent pegs in on a campsite without any hookups is what qualifies as dry camping. Real boondocking, on the other hand, has no hookups to any kinds of service and never occurs on a developed campsite. It is self-contained making you self-sufficient, so it does not necessarily mean that you will be going without.

Dispersed Camping

Dispersed camping often occurs in loosely controlled areas and can be free of charge. This style of outdoor recreation may be allowed in national parks for a small fee with certain limitations regarding where you are allowed to camp.

The defining factor of dispersed camping is that it is off the beaten track, away from designated camping grounds, and often far from other campers. These attributes are what make it impossible to be dependent on any service through the duration of your stay, and thus it is a better description of boondocking. If it were not for the fact that boondocking is only possible with an RV, then it would be the same thing.

How Do You Know You're Boondocking?

Since no bus service runs to the favored boondocking areas, you are going to need transport of your own. At this point, the importance of an RV is clear.

All boondocking is only such if it involves an RV that should be equipped to fulfill all your basic daily needs. With this vehicle, you should be able to cook, wash, sleep, and perform other essential functions. On your RV, there should also be a means to store your food in a manner that preserves it, with facilities to cook it and clean up after yourself. The average modern-day RV will have ablution facilities that consist of both a shower and a flushing toilet.

Most late-model RVs have TVs, microwaves, washing machines, etc. These appliances are not essential to the boondocking experience but are indicative of just just how advanced the hobby has become.

While on a long journey, you may need to charge batteries and run certain appliances and so you park in an area that has an electrical pedestal. True boondocking is without any hookups whatsoever. Furthermore, there should be no sign of civilization as far as the eye can see (due to the growth in the culture, this will exclude other RVers) and you should be surrounded by nature.

Be that as it may, it does not mean that if you find the remnants of an old cooking fire you are not boondocking. For conservation reasons, it is advisable to use these old parking sites as opposed to creating a new one. This is a common regulation when using areas managed by the U.S. Forestry Department or Bureau of Land Management (BLM).

Who Can Enjoy Boondocking?

Everybody can enjoy this form of recreation, but it requires that you have an affinity for nature. Since boondocking centers around a vehicle with a complex electronic and mechanical system, you do, however, need to have a certain degree of technical savvy. Boondocking is not like residing at a Holiday Inn or lodge in that it requires a hands-on approach, even if nothing needs repairing.

The RV is multifaceted, consisting of electrical, structural, and mechanical aspects. Boondocking demands that you be sharp and alert and constantly aware of what is happening with your rig.

Your journey will often take you far from any form of support. As an RVer, your responsibilities increase. Aside from technical issues and mechanical failures, you will also need to pay attention to your surroundings as mishaps born of nature are not unheard of.

The ability to navigate and a general sense of direction are good skills to have. Yes, getting lost may be part of the adventure, but every adventure should come to an end after a while.

Common sense is a big requisite. Nobody will be able to write down everything you should do when boondocking. You will have to learn some things as lessons and other things you will have to wing it by making decisions based on your ability to reason. As time goes on, you will get better at it. You will gain the experience and eventually become intuitive, often not knowing why you make certain judgments. As time goes on, more and more of these judgment calls will have favorable outcomes. Until then, be vigilant and learn.

Chapter 2

Preparing for the Journey

Do you know what you are getting yourself into? The answer to that cannot always be yes, even for outdoor veterans. Many a boondocker embarks on a journey with a spirit of adventure and in so doing he or she vies to discover the unknown.

So how do you prepare for the unknown? The best way to do it is with an open mind, as then you will be better primed for developments along your journey.

No Battle Plan Survives the Battle

There may be situations that you would rather not deal with. You can get a flat en route, which will result in you changing a tire in the rain, or the failure of your onboard stove, which forces you to cook over the fire. To make things interesting, there is often the need for something you have never done before.

There is a lot that can go awry when you are in the sticks and that is what preparation is for. The proverbial textbook filled with the experiences of those who went before you will show you how, but it does not have the answers to everything.

There are lessons that you will have to learn by yourself and the experience gained from these instances will make you eligible to add to the unwritten how-to manual of outdoor escapades.

If your mind is right, every event planned or not, will be an opportunity to build character, experience, and knowledge, while adding to your collection of anecdotes.

Research

While you cannot foresee all of the events that will affect your trip, researching your planned itinerary can help you create a favorable outcome. Scour the web and look for pictures, pore over maps, calculate distances, and get weather forecasts for the areas you plan on visiting. Get actual maps and study them, look at the towns that are proximal to your destinations, and see what services are available. Plan your drive days and departure times. Look out for areas with resupply opportunities and make notes of areas that will have a place for an emergency layover.

When you arrive in towns or stop over for supplies, speak to the locals. Find out as much as possible about the surrounding areas and the place you plan on parking for the night. Locals often possess knowledge that you will not find in guides or brochures.

The quality of your planning and research will determine your experience, so plan well, but be ready to improvise.

Food

Before shopping for food, design a menu. Plot out what you will eat every day. Try to be as specific as possible as spontaneity will only work when there is excess. In the case of boondocking, storage space is limited, as is the amount of food that can be brought along.

Meat planning and cold storage are critical areas of your planning. It is advisable to pre-freeze any meats that will go boondocking with you. Note that white meats become dangerous when cold storage is insufficient, and thus should be eaten as soon as they thaw out. Red meats like beef are inclined to age, so while it is still a priority to keep the latter adequately cold, it is not as crucial as white meat.

The fresh produce you bring along should be kept in a cool place, too. Depending on where you are headed and what the resupply opportunities are along your itinerary, you may have more than your fridge can hold. Things like vegetables should be stored in the coolest part of the vehicle. If it is a built-in storage box, perhaps it can be insulated and ventilated. Any place above the wheels is not appropriate and should be avoided because the tires generate heat when the vehicle is in motion.

Some of the most capable rigs can go for 14 days without a resupply. Note that during this time, you will very likely run out of fresh produce. To prevent anything from going to waste, you will need to use up perishables first and then resort to nonperishable foods. The only way to maintain adequate nutrition during this period is to buy dry goods, canned goods, and legumes. The latter may call on your creativity and culinary prowess when preparing meals.

Water

This is a vital part of your inventory. Incorrect planning in this area will leave you with a disaster. When going away for a prolonged period of time, make sure that you have enough water.

What is enough? What you think will be enough plus a bit extra. As is the case with everything else, space is a challenge. So while you may have water tanks built into your RV, take along extra drinking water. If you can find a natural and clean water source close to your boondocking spot, all the better. If you are unsure of the water, do not drink it; instead, boil it or use it for washing and cleaning.

An additional way to save water is by pre-washing all your fruit and vegetables when in areas with abundant water.

Electricity Alternatives

Stock up on energy alternatives. Devices that generate heat draw a lot of power and alternatives should be used where possible. Cook on gas or fire and take along a kettle that can be warmed over a wood flame. Instead of using the microwave to defrost frozen foods, take them out of cold storage way ahead of time and leave them out to thaw (place in the sunlight if necessary).

Prepping for Cold Weather

If you are planning a trip into cold weather, then cold storage will no longer be too big of a concern. The challenge is then keeping warm. The average RV wall is 2.5 inches thick and this is hardly a defense against the marauding cold of North American winters. Heating then becomes a priority.

Cloud coverage makes solar power an unreliable option and thus power conservation becomes even more critical.

There are multiple ways to fend off the cold. With the correct measures, your RV can be a cozy habitation irrespective of the weather outside.

Insulation and Waterproofing

One way to conserve heat is by adding a layer of insulation to your RV's walls. Not all RVs have insulated walls and in extreme temperatures, this lack becomes telling. There is a way to remedy this, but it can be quite labor-intensive. It entails stripping the interior of your vehicle and then adding the insulation against the outer aluminum wall. This insulation could be fiberglass, rigid foam, or spray foam. Additionally, there are foil-based options on the market and they are quite effective.

RV insulation is a technical task that requires an appropriate skillset. Keep in mind that you will be negotiating electrical cables, water pipes, and gas conduits. A mistake could make the job a lot more complicated than you have bargained for. If you are doing it yourself, the best way to go about the project is by doing one panel at a time. Done correctly, it will mitigate the cold of winter and the heat in summer. Do not forget the floor, as this can only be accomplished with an aftermarket product called RV skirting.

When covering windows, thermal curtains work well for keeping out the cold. They are not the only option though, as foil sheets and cardboard will work as well.

Heating

As mentioned, heat draws a lot of electricity and, for this reason, using power as a heating source is not a viable option. This is especially true if you are going to be off the grid for an extended period.

An RV's built-in heating system is normally powered by electricity or propane. Sometimes it even uses gas from the fuel tank. This can prove quite costly. It is for this reason that many seek out alternatives.

In winter, the vents on an RV can permit drafts and should be covered and insulated. The best form of insulation is styrofoam. It is a substance that is easily cut to fit and can be stuck over the vents with a mild adhesive or sticky tape.

Consider getting a wood stove for your camper. These are available in modern designs making them a lot safer than propane and diesel heaters. It works out cheaper in the long run.

There is always a danger of your pipes freezing over in winter and for this reason, there is a product called RV skirting.

The RV skirting is an innovation that separates the column of air underneath the RV from the colder encompassing air and thus prevents the pipework from freezing. The material used in this insulation can range from vinyl to rigid foam board. Common ways to attach skirting to the side of an RV is with snap fasteners, which may need drilling or in more user-friendly instances, just use adhesive or velcro. There are also the twist-lock fasteners that work best with fabric skirting.

While most skirting applications tend to be DIY jobs, there is a rather interesting option available on the market, namely the inflatable skirt. It is a pontoon-like device that you pump full of air and jam under the outer perimeter of your RV. The product has reinforced seams with heavy-duty valves and is made of weather and puncture-resistant material. The entire process of setting up these pontoon-like devices is said to take no more than 30 minutes (Airskirts LLC, 2021). When these items are no longer in use, they store easily as they can be deflated, rolled up, and packed away.

In severely cold weather, some feel it is necessary to place a heater behind the skirting and under the RV. For the sake of safety, this should not be a gas, propane, or diesel heater. The best heater for the job is a laser heater. If the heater falls over, it will switch off automatically.

Lighting

Out in the middle of nowhere, there is no light other than moonlight (if there is some on the night in question) and the stars. These celestial entities provide enough visibility where there is no light pollution. However, if there is a cloud cover, the darkness will become impregnable. For these instances be sure to take along at least two exterior lights that are powered by independent power sources. These lights may be pedestal mounted or attached to the side of your RV. Flashlights are essential, so make sure you have more than one that is reliable.

The Mechanical Aspects

The mechanical aspects of an RV are vitally important. When preparing for your off-grid experience, ensuring everything under the hood is as it should be is of the utmost importance. Make accommodation for things like engine oil, spare fuel, air filters, hose clamps, zip ties, and a fully outfitted toolbox. Every vehicle has a spare wheel but because of the nature of the driving you are going to be doing, customizing your RV to carry two spare wheels would be prudent.

Before every trip double-check that you have your tire iron, a working bottle jack, and a solid block of wood to serve as a base plate for the jack. These are priority and permanent features on your vehicle and should be inspected before every trip.

Ideally, vehicles should go to an auto shop before every long journey. This becomes even more of a priority when an RV has high mileage.

Navigation

The digital navigation available comes in the form of the traditional Global Positioning System (GPS) and mobile apps. As you may know, GPS depends on satellite coverage and, for this reason, these items are susceptible to signal interference and attenuation. This is why you should always have a map of the area you will be traveling to. Map reading is a necessary skill, so take the time to familiarize yourself with map symbols.

Learn how to navigate. Buy a compass and learn how to determine direction without a compass. Familiarize yourself with one or two constellations in the night sky and understand how to reference them for direction. Master the analog watch method for determining north.

You absorb this knowledge because it may one day get you out of a sticky situation, and every self-respecting outdoorsman should know a version of these skills.

Chapter 3

Urban and City Docking

Not all docking is boondocking. There are different places that you can park your RV and they range from parking lots to designated campsites. People often make use of inner-city parking spaces for stopovers on long journeys. These are also great places to fix, replace, and resupply.

Places to Park in Built-Up Areas

At times, you will need to spend the night proximal to or in a built-up area. It is always better to inquire about a spot before making a decision. It is a precaution that will mitigate the risk of you getting towed, fined, or having your rig broken into while you sleep. While many strict laws are governing the business and central areas, there are still places to park your RV at night.

Wally Docking

Another name for an overnight stay in a Walmart parking lot is Wally Docking. While not many people plan an overnight stay in a parking lot, it is likely to become necessary at some point in every boondockers' life. The need to dock at a supermarket chain is often brought on by imposing weather, mechanical failure, or one of the numerous other unforeseen circumstances.

Walmarts are usually situated in central areas. While these complexes allow docking, note that you will be off the grid too as there are no electrical or water hookups available. For this reason, an overnight stay in a Walmart parking lot is normally due to the lack of venues with the required RV amenities.

Wally Docking is widely practiced and Walmarts in rural areas tend to be more lenient about their parking lots. Once again, enquiring for permission is the best way to avoid being towed.

Mooch Docking

This is not a very nice term. The docking part of the term comes from boondocking, while mooch has connotations of an urchin or beggar. A better way of describing this practice would be Driveway Surfing. It often happens when you stopover on your itinerary to visit somebody.

Depending on the relationship and understanding with the driveways' owner, this can range from the length of one night to a few weeks. Since your RV is in the driveway, you are constantly in the spotlight and often are obligated to socialize with your hosts. This obligation can be an advantage, but if you like your privacy, it will quickly become a disadvantage.

The benefits of such a stayover are that most times mooch docking is free. With the help of an extension cord, you will have full electrical functionality and the chance to recharge your batteries. You might as well use the opportunity to refill your water tanks. Depending on how you are getting along with your hosts, you may be allowed to have a proper shower inside the house.

Docking on Developed Campsites

There are a fair amount of developed campsites that are near to business centers and this is ideal for RVers looking to experience the magic of a new city. These campsites normally charge a fee and require that you make a reservation beforehand. Being developed, they have electrical pedestals, spigots to top up your water, ablution facilities, and sometimes even WiFi. Not every RV camp is secure and some are hotspots for theft and break-ins. To avoid landing up at one of the bad ones, you should research them beforehand.

Camping at Undeveloped Campsites

Docking at an undeveloped camp is another form of off-grid living. These campsites are normally in national parks, forests, and lands run by the Bureau of Land Management (BLM).

They are rustic campsites and are available across the U.S., but because they are free, minimal effort goes into maintaining them. You would be lucky to find a working spigot at one of these.

Blacktop Boondocking

Blacktop Boondocking is when you park at a tar-surfaced rest-stop. In most cases, you are only allowed to stopover for one night. There are no hookups here and this is ideal for a single night's rest along a long journey. Look out for the no camping signs and if there is one, it means you cannot stay there overnight.

Another thing about rest-stops along highways is that the closer they are to big cities, the greater the likelihood of interaction with other people and who is to say whether or not they will be unsavory. There is no need to find out the hard way, so try to arrange something like a designated parking area in the city or drive until you find someplace more rural.

Truck Stops

These areas accommodate RVers overnight in the same manner that they do truckers. Sometimes, there are spots reserved for RVs, and while there may be an opportunity to top up with water, electrical hookups are not guaranteed. These spots will normally have a store, a filling station, and washing-up facilities for a small fee. Be sure to park in a manner that does not obstruct the big rigs.

Visitor Centers

RVers are normally allowed to park at visitor centers overnight. Before committing, get permission.

Trailheads

There are always cars parked overnight at trailheads, so an RV parked at such a location would not be out of place. The parked cars likely belong to backpackers who are spending the night on the trail.

Motel and Hotel Parking Lots

Large hotels with empty parking lots are worth the try. Confirm with security or management before committing so that you do not get towed.

Casino Parking lots

There are dedicated gamblers who game all night so there will always be cars in a parking lot. You may be required to register and park in a dedicated RV lot. Most casinos have a restaurant, so if you're looking for a hot meal you are likely to be in luck. These parking lots are for patrons though, so be sure to go in and show some aspect of the establishment some patronage. Some casinos have a full array of RV amenities.

Residential Areas

If you have to stop in a residential area, make sure it is a working-class suburb. These folk tend to be too wrapped up in their own lives to care about somebody squatting at the side of the road for the night. The best way to go about this in a built-up area is to pull in after dark and leave before first light.

Places Not to Overnight With Your RV

There are some places that you should not park when in a built-up area. The consequences that ensue will likely cause discomfort that you would rather do without.

On the Shoulder of the Road

Highways and roads carrying long-haul traffic are dangerous for stationary vehicles, period. The shoulder of the road is no place for parking overnight. It puts you in danger of being hit by vehicles that are moving on the side of the road or drivers who are not alert. It can end tragically, so avoid it at all costs.

Near Schools or Playgrounds

Parents are hyper-alert for anything that might pose a threat to their young. Strange vehicles with drawn blinds might be interpreted as such a threat. What this may result in is a visit from the police, a search, and if your right to be parked there is not 100% legitimate, you'll get a fine with marching orders.

Avoid these embarrassing situations where possible.

Sketchy Neighborhoods

Unless you are lulled to sleep by the sound of violence and gunfire, keep out of these neighborhoods. The riff-raff in these areas are good at spotting outsiders and often prey on them. An RV standing by itself late at night may be just too much of an opportunity to pass up.

Upper-Class Neighbourhoods

Upper-class areas, on the other hand, are also a harassment risk. People in these neighborhoods tend to be finicky and suspicious. They are likely to call the neighborhood watch or the police on you if they feel that your vehicle is standing around for too long. If the responding authorities deem fit, your vehicle may be liable for a search and perhaps a fine too, depending on their mood.

Opportunities to Empty Your Tanks

After a stint in the boonies, getting rid of blackwater is a priority. Out in the sticks dumping blackwater is physically possible but prohibited. The only place where it is permitted is in areas with a certain amount of infrastructure. Thus you will have to return to civilization and built-up areas to rid yourself of this waste; perhaps it is the first stop you will want to make. There will be many opportunities in the towns proximal to boondocking hot spots.

RV Showrooms

While not in the showroom per se, it will likely form part of the adjoining services that a dealership offers. Bear in mind there is probably going to be a fee involved.

Stores Selling Outdoor Gear

This is not a mandatory feature for outdoor adventure stores but there are a few franchises that offer these services to RVers. They do this in an attempt to add value to a customers' experience. These services may be free or otherwise conditional upon the purchase of goods from said stores.

Campgrounds That Are RV Friendly

If a campground welcomes RVers, then there is a fair chance that it has the facilities to dispose of wastewater.

National and Nature Parks

Not all parks offer this service, and it is thus advisable that you call ahead. Due to their proximity to the great outdoors, these are not normally a distance from the cities but there may be outlying towns that are close to these government-run conservations.

Filling Stations

Specifically truck stops and gas stations near recreation areas are among the places that allow you to get rid of your waste. Once again, if they advertise that they are RV friendly, then they will have everything you are going to need as an RVer.

Marinas

Boats have the same sanitary needs as RVs. For this reason, marinas have waste disposal solutions. Chucking blackwater into the marina is not a solution and will get you fined.

Water Treatment Facilities

These are often the sewage facilities that services households connected to the grid. Going directly to them is a rather more responsible action as they provide eco-friendly solutions for blackwater disposal (mind the smell, though).

Rules to Remember When Docking in a Built-Up Area

Think of your RV as a beast of freedom. No animal from the open plains can thrive in the city, as it is not its natural habitat. The city knows this of the RV and is not a tolerant host. So for the times you are in one with your RV, there are a few guidelines you need to follow if you want to stay out of trouble.

Always Get Permission First

The alternative is realizing that you are not allowed to park in a certain area when you get evicted in the middle of the night.

Respect the Parking Space

It is not a campsite. Do not unpack the barbecue, beers, or the deck chairs. Do not use the auto levelers as they cause damage to the surface of the parking bay. Stay self-contained, as you are only there to sleep.

Follow the Rules

These may change from state to state, so make sure that you are conversant with the regulations of the state that you are in.

If You Feel Unsafe, Don't Stick Around

Listen to your intuition. Sometimes it is all you have to go by.

Phone Ahead

If you are not sure if a certain establishment will allow you to park or have the amenities that you are after, phone ahead. Your experience is always easier if you know what to expect.

Keep Your Stay to Minimum

Docking in the city is not what your RV is intended for. The rules and regulations in place do not favor you as a boondocker, or your RV. The safest place for you is in transit on the highway or the hinterland.

Chapter 4

The Right Vehicle for the Job

There are a variety of different vehicles on the market varying in prices, sizes, brands, functions, and modes. Choosing one may be an exciting task, but it is not to be taken lightly. The choice you make here needs to be viable for a range of different reasons, and to serve its purpose to the fullest, the vehicle needs to check all the boxes.

Choosing Your RV

When in the recreation market, these are the things that need consideration.

Where Do You Plan on Going?

How long will your drives be and will they take you off the beaten track across rugged terrain? This will influence the size and weight of the RV you will need. If you plan on reaching those areas that are not too accessible, you may need to compromise on comfort and luxury for vehicle capability with an emphasis on agility and power.

How Big Is Your Family (Dogs Included)?

The size of your RV will have to be proportionate to that of your family. When thinking space, be sure to count the dogs because you will have no option but to let them sleep inside on those holidays in cold locations.

Do You Have a Big Enough Tow Vehicle?

If you are considering a fifth wheel, do you have a truck that can pull it? Is the truck big and strong enough for the job? (Montana, 2015)

How Good Are Your Parking Skills?

If your parking skills are questionable, avoid big rigs. They are difficult to maneuver and a nightmare to park in urban areas. If, however, you have no problem with the parking constraints of a big RV and prefer the inside space that they offer, then a large rig may be just the thing you are looking for.

What Will be the Length of Your Trips?

If it is a hobby that you will be enjoying for the duration of a two-year sabbatical, you would be more inclined to buy used. If it is a whole new lifestyle that you are going to take on in your retirement, then the better option would be a new RV.

Which Features of Your Normal Life Would You Like to Include?

Since the RV is just a miniaturized version of your home, you will want to take certain things with you. For instance, if you are passionate about French cooking, then you are likely to practice a version of this in the boonies, too. As such, all those ingredients will have to come along. If you enjoy beer, you may need extra cold space for storage.

What Is Your Budget?

Ultimately, this is the deciding factor: Based on your wallet, what are your options? Are you set up for big and luxurious or small and practical? Let's assume that you can comfortably afford the fifth wheel. Great. Do you have the truck that's needed to pull it, and if you do not, can you afford to buy that, too (Montana, 2015)?

Will You be Buying on Hire Purchase?

This is also a major consideration. Do not take a vehicle that is worth your entire monthly installment. Factor in fuel costs, park fees, repairs, and spares as part of your new recreational budget (Montana, 2015). If done correctly, you will not have to skimp on any adjoining expenses once you have purchased the vehicle.

Who Are the Designated Drivers?

A lot more goes into the decision-making process when there are multiple designated drivers. What size vehicle is everybody comfortable driving? Take RVs for test drives to establish this and see which handles best for all (Montana, 2015).

What Aspects of Boondocking Do You Intend on Prioritizing?

What are your needs? Are you happy to rough it here and there and make do without certain things? Or do you need certain aspects of your RV to be more developed (like your workspace)? This will determine the level of luxury and investment you will pursue when choosing an RV.

The above-mentioned are all factors that will help you decide on the correct rig (Montana, 2015).

The Most Common RVs

All RVs are not equal, not in size, capability, or maneuverability. People prefer different vehicles for different reasons, but of the many options available on the market, there are a few favorites.

Motorhomes

Motorhomes are defined by their fixed design where the engine and its accommodation aspects are part of the same unit.

This style of RV is available in three different classes: A, B, and C. These classes are mainly indicative of size.

A Class A RV has a resilient, sturdy frame that is built on a bus, truck, or motor vehicle chassis. These campers tend to be spacious with a minimum of two slide-outs and are also uncompromising on luxury. Fuel economy is close to non-existent as it slurps up a gallon for every nine miles it travels.

Class B motorhomes are almost the complete opposite of Class A. They are lighter without slideouts and a comparatively small interior. These are commonly known as camper vans and have a better fuel economy than its rather decadent cousin.

Last but not least, there is the Class C motorhome. It is easily recognizable by its over-cab extension (which accommodates a bed). This particular Class of RV is a combination of Classes A and B. It can tow a vehicle allowing for mobility without the risk of losing your campsite once you reach your destination.

The benefits of the motorhomes are that they are a unit and consume less space than trailers. The downside is that not everybody can travel with two cars and this means that should you want to skip into town, you would have to break up camp and risk having it snatched up before you return.

Truck Campers

Truck campers (TC) refer to an aluminum or fiberglass box that is carried on the back of a truck. It has a cabover section that accommodates a sleeping area, windows, and often slide-outs. A TC has all the capabilities of an RV and can fulfill its functions with an added quality of agility and mobility thanks to the truck aspect.

This kind of RV is perfect for accessing those remote locations with bad driving conditions.

The one disadvantage of the CT is its limited interior space, which makes it unsuitable for a family.

Travel Trailers

Travel trailers are favored for their stand-alone capability. Attached to a decent truck, this type of RV is easy enough to haul and it allows the occupants and owner to leave it behind once a camp has been chosen and set up.

When Looking to Buy

Never buy an RV without seeing it first. Make sure you have the opportunity to walk through it and physically examine every facet of it. Do not make payments without doing the walk-through, no matter how good a deal seems to be. If it sounds too good to be true, it normally is.

When choosing an RV, there is so much more to check for than a normal vehicle. A thorough inspection is necessary irrespective of whether the vehicle is new or used. Used RVs require knowledge and experience in the same area and thus it is best to take along someone who knows what to look for.

There are typically occurring issues to look out for on second-hand RVs.

Mold

Mold is a sure sign of moisture that is caused by water leaks. Brown run marks on the ceiling are also clear indicators of moisture issues.

Leaks

Water leaks can have a knock-on effect, and where there are signs of water, you should look for rotting wood, rusting metal, and faulty electronics.

Floor Damage

Creaking floorboards attest to damaged floors. It may not impress the salesman, but feel free to take a flashlight and scrutinize the underbelly of the vehicle.

Exterior

Examine the walls for integrity and look for water stains, holes, and other areas where moisture may invade.

Electronics

This is a very sophisticated aspect of an RV, and when doing an inspection, it is advisable to have somebody with knowledge in the field along for a consultation.

The Roof

The roof is an important aspect of your RV, so you want to be pedantic about your scrutiny of it. Once again, any signs of mold or water stains are sure indicators of moisture and leaks.

Who to Buy From?

Admittedly, some private sales are bargains provided you know exactly what you are paying for, but the problem is that you never really know. The best way to go about this business is to buy from a reputable reseller who has a reputation to maintain. It will mitigate the chances of hidden issues and you are likely to get a warranty. It will work out a bit more expensive but think of it as the price of dependability.

Chapter 5

Safety First

Boondocking should be as free of stress and anxiety as possible. Employing the necessary measures to avert any catastrophe threatening to rob you of your fun will give you this peace of mind.

The adage, safety first, is not just a saying but the main priority in RVing. Taking the correct safety measures will allow you longevity and the ability to continue doing what you love.

Personal and Vehicle Safety

Safety considerations are what stops many people from partaking in the hobby. The fear of what might happen along the way and the reputation of unsavory humans contribute to these considerations. Additionally, it is the angst for what hides in the dark outside the RV in the dead of the night when 100 miles from any kind of help.

While these reservations are natural, veteran boondockers will tell you that it wears off after a while. That being said, there are always precautions that you should take.

The main aspect of your safety is your personal being, the second, your RV. On a trip, you are dependent on your RV for safety and survival and thus your safety and that of your RV are for most parts the same thing. To preserve this safety, there are ways to mitigate the chances of a bad experience.

Follow Your Intuition

Depending on your instincts is often all you have to go on. The feeling that a place or person gives you should not be dismissed. Be attentive to the alarm bells in your head, when RVing, as you will be dependent on your own devices.

Share Your Coordinates

With every stop, share your location in the form of an address or coordinates with a relative or family member. If you know where you will be going the next day, share this with relatives or friends, too.

When boondocking alone, avoid walking too far from your campsite. If you want to take a walk, make sure that there is nothing that can hamper your return and that you always have a clear line of sight to your RV.

Take a Mobile With You

Set a check-in schedule with someone back home and adhere to it religiously. That can be anywhere between once a day to every three days. This will take some effort if you are going out of cellular network range. If you have the means, take along a satellite phone.

Stash It, Don't Flash It

Hide your valuables. Unnecessarily showing off draws attention and often the kind attention that you would rather not have. Keep the amounts of money on you down to a minimum.

Lock Your Doors

Open doors and windows are like an invitation to marauders. Make sure that your RV is properly locked up when you are away from it or asleep. This is even more important when parked in towns.

Keep Your Valuables Packed Away

Many smash-and-grab crimes occur because of valuables left in plain sight. This can easily be avoided by drawing the blinds or covering up windows. When your lights are on, people on the outside will be able to see in, but you will not be able to see out. For this reason, it is also advisable to keep the blinds drawn at night.

Follow Reviews

There are review websites discussing outdoor camping locations, products, and service providers. While the BLM or National Parks may advertise places as idyllic and safe, the information that you need is best provided by former patrons or individuals who have had first-hand experiences. Use reviews rather than advertisements to make a decision.

Talk to Locals

Arrive in town early, dock in a parking lot, and spend a few hours at a diner. If you like it there, start a few conversations. Bear in mind, though, that small-town inhabitants can be notoriously suspicious and territorial. Also, be aware of the people around you and learn to read the mood.

Nobody knows an area better than the locals. The local cops may be helpful or critical and suspicious. Bartenders and waiters are valuable sources, and there is nothing like a good tip to loosen their tongues.

Park Out of Site of the Main Drag

Where permitted, try to pick a boondock site that is not visible from the main road. By doing it this way, you will not attract unwanted attention. RV raiders and predators (in human form) would be more likely to target campsites and RV parks anyways. Taking additional precautions while in the sticks will not hurt. If you are out of sight, you are out of mind.

Pack Bear Spray

Bear spray is effective for fending off animals of the two-legged or four-legged variety. Some boondockers prefer taking along a firearm. If this makes you feel safe, then do so.

Safety in Numbers

Even if the entities pushing your headcount up are your two dogs, they will still count. The more military-trained humans you take with, the greater the deterrent to unsavory characters who might want to come snooping around your camp.

Make Friends with Your Neighbors

While you do not want to walk a path in the grass between your RV and your neighbors' setup, it is always good to lift a hand in acknowledgment, and if the response is enthusiastic, go over for a brief chat. By doing this, you will establish your presence and make an impression. Should an emergency arise later, your neighbors will feel obliged to help you.

Staying Self Contained

Keeping it all on board as much as possible does not only have organizational value but it allows you to leave quickly. To allow for this, be sure to wash up and pack everything before bedtime. This way, if the need arises, you can leave during the night or early in the morning as it will not take you long to get moving.

Scout the Area Around Your Site

Look out for things that may become hazardous to your intended campsite. If you are in the rain, be wary of areas that may become boggy and prohibit thoroughfare on your way out. In the same circumstances, avoid dry washes that may become rivers and flash floods, or being near anything that can be affected by a mudslide. Keep your eyes peeled for signs of previous mudslides and avoid these areas in rainy conditions.

Make sure that there is more than one exit to your camping area and, if possible, park in a manner that allows you to access without difficulty.

Pay Attention to All Your Senses

If you smell smoke in the area, it means there is a fire. Is it a cooking fire that you smell? If it is, what does this mean? Very likely other humans are trying to figure them out if possible.

Can you smell burning vegetation? Is the sky cloudy on the horizon? Is it a forest or prairie fire? Which direction is the wind blowing and is the direction likely to change? Will it pose a danger to you eventually?

Make decisions early and take preemptive action.

Bear Proof Your RV

Animals are attracted by strong smells, so try to keep the pungent cosmetics down to a minimum. Make sure that your food is packed away and dispose of scraps far from camp. If you have the mind to, bury your food scraps so that the smell will be stifled, and be sure to bury them away from your campsite, too.

Do Not Single Yourself Out

Things like custom vinyls and stickers are what make people remember you, keep them to a minimum. When traveling alone, the idea is not to stand out but to blend in.

Keep a discreet hiding place on your RV for valuables like contingency money, credit cards, backup mobiles, etc.

Road Safety

An RV is a composition of two main facets. One is the accommodation aspect and the other is mobility. For these two to operate in tandem, they both need to be on par, checked, and catered for with the same level of priority.

The mechanical aspects of your RV have the same requirements as a normal motor vehicle. Except for towed RVs, they may need to be monitored more closely and serviced more frequently because of the long distances they travel.

Fuel Planning

On a long journey, your fuel stops should be planned way ahead of time. Before taking the high road, make sure that you are at capacity. If you have a backup tank and jerry cans, you can fill them, too, as long as they are a safe means of storage and not a fire hazard. Store your jerry can out of the way and, if it is mounted outside, make sure that it is theft-proof.

Your fuel level should never be allowed to drop below a quarter in the main tank when all other tanks are empty.

Built-in backup tanks are normally connected to the main tank. Dual-tank fuel systems use an electric pump to transfer gas and this is either an automated process or can be manipulated from inside the cab. Some setups have a valve along with the connecting hose that needs to be opened and closed manually. The hose linking them usually transfers fuel using gravity or osmosis and these kinds of systems are the most basic of aftermarket customizations. Backup tanks come in handy if you would like to make fewer stops along your itinerary.

Jerry cans should be filled once at the beginning of a journey and only used in the event of an emergency. It should not be factored in as part of your fuel inventory.

If you do not feel safe about traveling with so much gas, then you can always fill up to capacity just before you go off the beaten track.

Oil

Your vehicle comes with a user manual that indicates how often you should change your oil. For most modern vehicles, it is between every 5,000 to 7,000 miles. For older vehicles, an oil change is needed every 3,000 miles. If your rig is using a fully synthetic lubricant, then it will likely need a change after every 15,000 miles (AAA Automotive, n.d.).

Each vehicle's needs depend on where the vehicle is used, how long they stand for, the age of the engine, the make, and the model. The condition of an engine's oil and how quickly it deteriorates are indicative of the condition of the engine, and thus the only way to stay abreast of an engine's condition is to check its lubricant. As a rule, oil should be checked before the start of every long journey.

Even if you do not change the engine oil, you should check it more often when on a long trip, and especially when you drive through different climates, altitudes, and temperatures. Towing also affects the way your engine performs and how it reacts to the lubricants you use.

Water

It is prudent to keep five gallons of water on the vehicle to top up when the engine requires it. Doing this will be especially useful if your car has a tendency to overheat. This normally happens to older cars. As a safety tip, make sure that your engine cools down properly before opening the radiator cap.

Lights

Before you get into your vehicle, check all your exterior lights. Make sure that they are working. If you are towing, check your trailer lights, too.

Drive with your headlights on during the day because it improves other road users' visibility of you and helps them see you from a distance.

Tires

Check your tire pressure and keep an eye out for slow punctures. Inspect the sidewalls and the tread for excessive wear or damage. Do the same for the spare wheels and try to equip with more than one per vehicle. When towing, exercise the same caution with trailers.

Windows and Mirrors

Make sure that windows and mirrors are clean so that you can see where you are going. Most vehicles come off the production line with a shatter-proof film. This is important as there are always flying stones that get kicked up by the wheels. Fix any pre-existing chips before they turn into cracks.

The Cab

Prep your cab for driving. Make it as comfortable as possible and minimize the potential for distraction. Keep a water bottle with a nozzle on hand, use your cupholder and get a hands-free kit for your mobile device. Place your snacks in a place that is easily accessible. Open wrappers and packaging before time and position them within easy reach.

Keep your footwell clear, bottles rolling around can get under the pedals and this is something you do not want to happen.

Maps

When driving, use a map that is app-based (on your mobile) and keep your mobile securely mounted to the windshield. Memorize the key landmarks on your route as indicated by your map. There are offline map services that require downloading and need no network to operate. Get these for the relevant state that you intend on driving through so that you are not left stranded when you run out of satellite or network connectivity.

Rest Regularly

The standard rest intervals are every two hours. Seasoned drivers can get by on longer drive times, but everybody is different. Remember that a lot more is at stake than just you and your rig. Think of the passengers in the vehicle with you, your fellow road users, and the higher level of responsibility that comes with towing a trailer. Rather err in the way of caution.

Another way to capitalize on drive time is to have more than one designated driver. By doing it this way, you can rotate the drive duty while making good time and both parties get turns to rest sufficiently

Avoid large meals when driving long distances as these tend to make you sleepy. Rather snack regularly as this keeps you active and awake.

Passengers

Make sure that all passengers are settled and belted in. This includes adults, children, and pets alike. In the case of animals, use the relevant cages, and for toddlers the appropriate baby seats. Anyone or thing that hampers your concentration increases the risk of a road accident.

Poor Driving Conditions

Rain, snow, and reduced visibility create poor driving conditions. Slick road surfaces reduce traction and increase the distance and time needed to stop. It is a lot easier to lose control of a vehicle when the weather is wet.

Weather apps are useful for planning your drive and itinerary. Newspapers at coffee shops and the news on TV at diners can be valuable resources, too.

Chapter 6

Minimize Your Footprint

There are a surprising number of ways to reduce your impact on nature when boondocking. Generally, it requires a conscientious approach with consistent behavior.

Boondock More Often

While boondocking does not automatically constitute greener living, it is so much closer to it and creates a great starting point. Responsible boondocking makes your holidays greener and thus you contribute to a healthier environment.

By disconnecting from the grid (water, electricity, and sewage) and relying on your limited resources, you are forced to consume conservatively. If however, you have to plug into an electrical pedestal at a park or elsewhere, you automatically go back onto the grid, and thus you are no longer as eco-friendly.

Today's RVs are generally built from composite materials and are more energy-efficient than ever. These vehicles are specifically designed to get by on limited resources.

There are a few ways that you can modify your RV to make it more efficient and minimize its carbon footprint.

Optimize and Manage Your Electronics

One of the first places you can start is by swapping all your lights for light-emitting diodes (LEDs). These draw less power and so you conserve more battery life.

Modern electrical appliances are more power-efficient than earlier models. Try to use newer model appliances or items that are energy efficient in your RV.

Get into the habit of turning off devices when you do not need them. TVs and radios in your vehicle can stay off when you are outside as well as the lights. Use this method so that necessary appliances like your fridge can run constantly.

Add Solar Panels

Solar panels are cheaper in the long run and they produce clean energy from the sun. In this case, as long as you have sunshine, you will have a power source. Calculate your power needs and get the appropriate number of panels. You could even install a bigger setup than you need as it is better than underestimating.

Use Smaller Faucet Nozzles and Shower Heads

These modifications will help you conserve water. Smaller shower heads need less water to create a pressured stream.

Recycle Graywater

Collect your shower water and use it to flush the toilet instead of using clean water. It will spare you space in your waste tanks and save freshwater.

Take Doug for a Walk

Get yourself a special shovel. Name it Doug (pronounced 'dug'). When nature calls, take him for a long walk to a private place. Make sure the paperwork for the transaction is biodegradable. Dig a hole, and when you are done, cover it up. Now you are living!

The aforementioned walk will save you flushing water and waste tank space.

Cook Over a Campfire

What a great excuse to barbecue, and if you get tired of barbecuing, then cook. Cooking over the campfire is a bit more labor-intensive than using gas or electricity, so you may not be up for the task every night. Once you start learning a few recipes and tricks (like building makeshift ovens) fire-cooking becomes fun. To be more prepared, you can practice your skills at home first.

Cooking over the fire need not be difficult and will save you both electricity and propane. You can use your barbecue or a campfire tripod. Just be sure to have a stoker close by and some oven gloves. All stirring utensils for these methods should be metal.

Set an Example

People are inspired by the actions of others. Take a garden rake with you and tidy your camp, make this the last thing you do before leaving your campsite. Tidy up the area you used for your cooking fire, leave no litter behind, and restore the area to the state that it was in when you arrived. If it was in a shoddy state because of the previous RVer, then leave it in a cleaner state. The idea here is to leave visible evidence that you have cleaned up so that the boondockers who come after you will feel obliged to do the same.

Take Everything You Brought Back with You

Do not leave anything behind at the campsite, except for the geocache you left behind when you took Doug for a walk. If the rubbish is too filthy to pack in the RV, wrap it in a black bag and then secure it to the outside of your rig. Consider getting a dedicated box that can be bear-proofed and attach it to the roof of the RV.

Buy fewer disposable containers and opt for things that you can recycle and use again. Another effective strategy for reducing waste is to remove excessive packaging before storing it in the RV.

Avoid Propane and Electricity for Heating

If the nights are cold, use extra comforters. Heat water over your cooking fire and fill a few empty soda bottles and screw the caps on tight. These can be placed at random points in the RV or even between the sheets. The next day, paint them black and stand them in the sun all day. The black paint will dry and absorb the sun's rays, warming the water. When the sun goes down, move them indoors and then back into the sunlight the next day.

If there is overcast weather, put these bottles around the cooking fire so that they will contact the heat from the flames. While this method may not be as effective as filling the bottles with boiling water, it is an efficient way of harnessing thermal energy.

An effective way to conserve heat is to block vents and insulate walls. Another way is to take the heated rocks from around the fire and wrap them in an old cloth and keep them in the RV. They will likely lose their heat faster than the water bottles, but for a time, they will help heat the RV.

When these fire-based innovations are not enough, resort to gas heaters and avoid depleting your electricity supply or starting your generator.

Parking

You may have noticed that when vegetation is deprived of sunlight for an extended period, it dies. When parked in a grassy area for more than a day, try moving the camper so that the area that the rig has shaded gets sunlight again.

Try to park in areas that previous RVers have used so that the impact of your presence on nature is minimal.

Be Fire-Wise

If there is a sign that says no fires, then do not make any fire. The reason the sign is there is because of the hazard created by a naked flame and the area's history with fires getting out of control.

If there are no fire prohibition signs, go ahead, but be careful, especially in windy circumstances. If there is wind and the environment of your site has a lot of dry vegetation, fire becomes a bigger hazard. If there is wind, but minimal organic fuel (dry vegetation) in the area, then get it going in a barbecue stand or an old ventilated metal drum, which you will have to bring along for this purpose.

Use your discretion but note that if the wind whips up excessive sparks once the fire is going, you might need to douse it. These sparks can ride the wind until they land on dry organic materials and that will be the start of a disaster.

Another way of getting a controlled fire going in windy circumstances is by digging a Dakota Fire Hole.

The first step of the process is to dig a hole under the overhang of a bush. The hole should be about eight inches wide, circular in shape, and about a foot deep. A foot upwind from this hollow, dig another that is eight inches wide with a tunnel slanting downwards towards the first hole. The ground between the two holes should remain intact.

You can circle the original pit with small rocks and then start a fire inside it. The wind blowing in through the second hole will help the fire catch and keep it lively. The flames need not exceed the hole.

By resting a barbecue metal grid either flat on the ground over the hole or on stones of equal height, you can create an even space for a pot or a kettle. The fire will remain undetected by anybody on level ground, and the smoke plumes will disintegrate through the leaves of the bush's leafy overhang. Make sure that the bush is still green and alive to help with the smoke. To cook a meal, you would have to sit on your haunches like the Dakota did when they made their fires.

Note that if the ground is moist enough, the hole can be created by scooping out the soil in a single chunk. By returning it to the fire hole intact all traces of the fire having ever been there will be obliterated.

Stay on the Beaten Track

Where your wheels roll, nature gets hurt. It is for this reason that you should stick to the beaten track where possible. The effect of a vehicle driving over the ground can have fatal consequences for any subterranean form of life. The weight of the vehicle makes tunnels cave in, collapses dens, and destroys the roots and stems of the vegetation below. In arid regions, a vehicle's tracks can have a destructive impact that will last a few centuries (Lalley & Viles, 2006).

Do Not Leave Food Outside

The scents of edibles to the keen nostrils of wild animals are sometimes too much to resist. Consistent behavior like this eventually leads to wild animals, like bears, associating humans with food. The results might include daring behavior by the wildlife and eventually aggression that sometimes leads to attacks on humans. The only solution for an aggressive animal is death.

Scenarios like this are recurrent and brought on by interactions between careless people and nature. Every incursion by humanity on nature has a domino effect.

Noise Is Pollution

Playing loud music, or even behaving in a boisterous manner, has no place in nature. It disrupts the ambiance and disturbs others who are out there for peace. Noise also disturbs wildlife and unsettles the natural routines of most animals. Acoustic disturbances that are borne of unnatural sources disrupt breeding cycles and, in the long run, endangers species. This is a threat that is likely to bring vulnerable animal life closer to extinction (Iberdrola, n.d.).

National parks and other conservation areas have noise restrictions in place to curb this kind of behavior. These regulations are difficult to enforce for the farther-flung areas. The responsibility then falls to the camper or boondocker to conduct him or herself in a manner that is respectful of the surroundings.

Chapter 7

The List of Everything You Will Need for Boondocking

If it is going to be your first rodeo, you are probably wondering where to start. There is no universal list for packing an RV and every trip's requirements depend on factors like personal taste, vehicle capabilities, and the intended length of the journey.

Some items are optional, but everything that aids the maintenance of the vehicle and general safety should be treated as mandatory. This chapter will guide you through the things you need to take with you when boondocking.

RV-Related Essentials

An RV, being self-contained, needs accessories to operate at its optimum capacity. The items that make up these necessities allow for the ease of operation, adaptability, and provide the measures to safeguard the rig from external factors.

Electrical Surge Suppressor

This device is important for those dodgy electrical pedestals at RV parks or charging points in general. Electrical surges are common in public areas caused by variables like heavy demand placing a strain on the grid. These scenarios often result in the electrical supply dropping and then surging. Electrical surges can also be caused by lightning, faulty appliances, and among other things, bad wiring.

There are different versions of surge protectors available on the market. The first factor influencing the choice you make will be according to the amp service your RV uses (30 amps or 50 amps). A 50-amp suppressor will work on a 30-amp outlet. A 30-

amp suppressor will prevent surges but reduce the 50-amp current to 30-amps if used on the former.

There are two ways of preventing an electrical surge. The first way comes in the form of a portable device. It is about as easy to carry as a six-pack of beers and is twice as effective and three times as coveted. Some high-end options have a built-in display, which with the help of an accompanying manual, is capable of giving you specifics of the electrical current flowing through it and if there are any discrepancies.

The portable surge suppressor connects directly to the external power source like the electrical pedestals in RV parks. Leaving it outside overnight is not recommended. These devices are highly valued among those who know what they are, and they tend to go missing quickly. This is the one con that outweighs all the pros.

The better option is the permanent surge suppressor. Certain models of this device may also serve as an electrical management system (EMS). The advantage of using this device is that it is secure and an integral part of an RV electrical system. These items are available in the highest levels of technological advancement, so much so that they can be monitored from mobile devices.

Electrical Plug Converters/Adapters

Electrical plug points differ from place to place. Two of the main variations at designated RV charging points are the 50-amp and the 30-amp service. There are unidentical plug sockets that carry different amperages. An advanced RV-friendly establishment will host one of each and an additional receptacle capable of carrying 20 amps.

To avoid disappointment, you should not assume this of every RV campsite but rather phone ahead and ensure that the fittings at the resort will accommodate your RVs shore plug. For moments when this is not possible, there are adapters. These electrical fittings make any amp service agnostic. If the service is insufficient, there are upgrades you can make to the electrical system to compensate for this (with a hybrid inverter).

Make sure you have adapters for every kind of power receptacle you can think of.

Toilet Chemicals

The types designed for RVs are not per se chemicals in that they are composed of organic enzymes with bacteria. These enzymes will assist in breaking down the human waste in toilets. The upside of these enzymes is that they also eliminate the smell caused by blackwater. Not all toilet additives are biodegradable. Be sure to use those designed for RVs as they are organic.

RV Sewer Hose Kit

These are available in all shapes, colors, and sizes. The function of a sewer hose serves to carry blackwater out of the RV to a drain. These pipes are made of plastic and reinforced with wire coils, and this combination makes them resilient and flexible. Sewer hoses are available with a variety of different fittings that allow you to connect them at angles that would otherwise be awkward.

The joints are available in 90- and 45-degree angles, and in transparent options (so you can see when your holding tanks are clean). There are also different sizes to adapt to different fittings.

There are even agnostic adapters that can screw or clip into different tank and sewer drain receptacles. Additionally, these kits are sold with leak caps that screw on to prevent moisture from dripping all over the storage space.

Not all sewer kits are of the same quality. Those pipes with thicker walls and joints are stronger and less likely to break, wear out, or leak.

Quick Dissolving Sanitary Paper

Standard domestic toilet paper can put a lot of strain on an RVs plumbing, for this reason, there are special kinds of sanitary paper that are biodegradable, dissolve quickly, and pose less of a clogging risk than the usual.

A Pressure Relief Valve

The pressure of water coming out of a domestic spigot is in the range of 40 psi and 60 psi (Becker, 2006). Although modern RVs are capable of handling up to 100 psi. Those in the know feel that if the water pressure is higher than 60 psi, it may be unhealthy for the RV plumbing system (Thiel, 2021).

Since there are no guarantees, the risk of connecting to a source with higher pressure is ever-present. A pressure relief valve serves to dilute the force with which water is let into an RV plumbing system. As such, this device avoids leaks, burst pipes, and other damages that high-pressure connections may cause.

Fresh Water Hose

The drinking water hose is vitally important. The longer the better, as you don't know where you will have to draw water from next. If detachable, store this hose in a different location from the RV's other plumbing (especially the sewer). The aforementioned pressure regulator will connect to one end of the hose.

Leveling Chocks

As a boondocker, you will often find yourself on rugged terrain. Whether or not your RV has auto levelers, you always need to travel with leveling chocks/blocks. While the auto levelers work fine on solid terrain, they are useless on desert sand or soft ground. The leveling blocks, which are primarily designed to go under tires, will effectively second as base plates for the auto levelers. The blocks are available in wood, plastic, and other synthetic materials.

Tire Pressure Checker

The RV, being a bigger-than-usual vehicle, bears a heavier load than most private motor cars. The tires need to be filled with the right amount of air so that the RV remains safe and fuel-efficient when in motion. Make sure that you test your air pressure gauge against others regularly (preferably high-quality gauges that are known to be accurate). The purpose of the latter is to ensure that your gauge is in good working order and giving you accurate readings.

A faulty gauge results in incorrect readings. The consequences may lead to blow-outs, which can be fatal.

Electrical Extension Cables

Having an electrical extension is a precaution. Every RV charging pedestal is placed in a position easily reached by the RV's native cabling. For the rare event that your RV does not have a long enough electrical cable, or the event that you charge from an undesignated source, an electrical extension cord will come in handy.

Shovel

Doug the geocacher will suffice. A shovel is an essential accessory for prolonged outdoor stays and should be part of the permanent inventory of an RV. They are handy for digging fire pits (like the Dakota firehole), clearing snow from campsites, and among many other things, digging out bogged-down vehicles.

Insulation and Gaffer Tape

Insulation tape is essential when rewiring or making repairs to cables. Gaffer tape is good to have around, too, especially for keeping things closed, taping up holes, and making temporary repairs.

You cannot predict what you might need an emergency solution. Gaffer tape can be used for a wide variety of things in various environments. It is adherent to most surfaces, water-resistant (though not entirely waterproof), and strong. It is especially useful as a temporary solution for smashed windows and loose auto lights.

Waterproof Airtight Containers

You'll need these containers not so much for food as for paperwork and documents. The best would be a Ziploc big enough so that it can hold IDs, licenses, registrations, and all your important paperwork that needs to remain dry and clean.

An Emergency Road Kit

Packing along an extra stash of goods may seem unnecessary, especially if duplicates of them recur throughout your main inventory of day-to-day essentials. If you are inclined to frequent remote locations that require long driving trips, an emergency road kit should be a priority.

Due to the isolated nature of boondocking, you will many times be far from humanity and thus you will be far from help should there be a demobilizing event. An emergency road kit is a basic compilation of gear and resources, along with tools and devices that can help you survive or prevent you from being stranded.

With that in mind, the things that go into this special inventory will be as follows.

Non-Perishable, Ready-to-Eat Food and a Few Days Supply of Bottled Water

Your emergency food does not form part of your regular inventory and should not be counted as such. It should be checked frequently for integrity but only be used in exigent circumstances.

Extra Clothing and Shoes

The wardrobe you pack for an unseen event may be adapted to where you will be traveling. If it is going to be hot, then you will pack cotton tops, sun hats, and light linen, but since the weather is not always predictable, it is prudent to also make preparations for the opposite. One change of winter wear should do the trick along with an extra thick blanket or two.

A Medical Box

Most vehicles come off the production line with first-aid kits. These are often very basic, so compiling your version would entail that you add to these kits making them more comprehensive. Make sure that among the usual items, there is a seatbelt cutter along with a windup flashlight and a waterproofed canister with candles and matches. Pack in some electrolyte kits because most ailments while out in the sticks are either caused or accompanied by dehydration.

A Breakdown Kit

Doug's other shoveling function will be to clear away soft sand or snow when getting a vehicle unstuck. For this purpose, traction mats are a necessity along with a length of tow rope. These are all items that you would need to get yourself out of a sticky situation with or without the help of another vehicle.

For scenarios like this, you can have a bumper winch installed. While it will look more aesthetic on a camper truck, it will be a lot more useful on a Class B or C motorhome. Its uses will be invaluable in the case of a bogged down RV far away from any rescue services. With the right tools, mindset, experience, and knowledge, there are not many scenarios that you will be incapable of rescuing yourself from.

Whistles, warning lights, road flares, and fire extinguishers all form parts of the breakdown inventory.

Booster Cables

Booster cables are a must-have because a great part of your RV is battery-operated. Should your starter battery run out, you will need to boost it with one of your RV batteries. Get the problematic battery replaced or serviced as soon as possible. The regular use of deep-cycle batteries to jump a car's motor may cause it damage, thus it is best to get the faulty starter battery fixed or replaced at the soonest possible opportunity.

Kitchen and Cooking Supplies

The management of your kitchen and cooking supplies will reflect on your entire experience. Out and away from all the usual distractions of urban life, food becomes a high point of your boondocking experience.

A Lot of Water

You can never have enough water. Prioritize it and decide what you would be happy to clean with, cook with, and drink. Take along extra jugs of drinking water.

Cooking Utensils

The contents of the RV kitchen are the downsized versions of everything you would use to cook in a home kitchen. The more of an outdoor experience you want, the less dependent you will be on electrical cooking appliances.

Webers, gas cookers, or barbecue stands can come along. Cutlery should not be disposable and no paper plates should make it into your wilderness getaway (boondocking is an eco-friendly adventure). If you don't want to bring the fine china along, then purchase stainless steel.

There is no need to downgrade the version of cutlery you bring, just make sure it is enough with one or two spare sets. Pack in the usual cutting knives, dishing spoons, and make sure they are all stainless steel. If you are going to be doing a lot of outdoor cooking, avoid plastic. Be sure to include a strong set of tongs.

Always pack wood for cooking and campfires. Not every location is fit for cooking and some conservations prohibit burning the wood that is in the area.

Do not forget your cleaning detail. Biodegradable dish soap, scourers, and non-disposable dish towels are necessary because you will be washing up and reusing them as opposed to throwing them away.

Staples and Foods

Many people recommend premixed batters and pre-processed foods. These are helpful for those long-driving days, but otherwise try to immerse yourself in the outdoor cooking culture. Make a point of using fire when permitted by the rules.

There are hundreds of recipes for some of the most delicious, healthy, and wholesome meals. These dishes can all be made from your RV or over a fire.

Campfires are not limited to cowboy meals. With good coals, cast-iron pots, and trial and error, you would be surprised at what you can bake. Remember practice makes perfect, so don't be disheartened by early results.

The ingredients you pack should be according to a predesigned menu. Take backup foods in case of kitchen disasters and unforeseen burnt offerings. The longer you plan on going without a supply run, the better your planning needs to be. Try to keep the trips between the supply runs regular at first. As you gain experience, you will be able to last longer without a trip to restock your inventory.

Meat is a must on this list. Take fish but only if you can keep it frozen until you use it.

The amount of fresh produce you take along will depend on the length of time you can keep it from going bad. Veggies like potatoes, carrots, and onions tend to last longer in dry environments with good ventilation, while tomatoes, lettuce, and cucumbers do not hold up in hot weather. Mushrooms, cauliflower, and broccoli are also examples of fresh produce that go bad quickly.

Fruit can be tricky in hot weather, so take along just enough to consume before it goes bad. When you run out, switch to canned fruits. The gist of the matter is this: The more cold space you have, the more fresh produce can go along. However, because most RVs are challenged for space, perishable foods need to be limited when out in the boonies for longer periods.

Just because you're off the grid does not mean that your food needs to be bland. Be sure to take along spices and condiments.

A backup supply of dry goods, legumes, canned foods, cereals, and non-perishables will fill the gap and create options. You will probably be snacking a lot, so pack accordingly.

Clothing and Bedroom Items

Take the correct clothing for the location you will be visiting and some for alternate weather, just in case. It is also a good idea to try and take with things that are quick-drying and comfortable to wear

Miscellaneous but Necessary

There are things that you would rather have with you despite your break from the grid. These include your mobile and the charger. Just because you decided to go on a social media fast does not mean that you do not need your phone. Sometimes you will need to make reservations and search for information that is crucial to your journey.

Credit Cards and Cash

Keep the cash hidden, break it into small denominations, don't flash it, and use it where cards are not accepted.

Spare Batteries

If you have the space and means, keep a replica of the battery under the hood stashed away, and a supply of new flashlight batteries in a cool dry place

Wrist Watch

The more functions it has, the better.

Medications

If you are on any prescriptions, take along enough medication and make sure that you have the means to contact medical help should the need arise.

Travel Map

Take a paper one that is relevant to the area you are going no matter what digital navigation you have in place. Where the digital fails, the analog will save the day.

Cosmetics

Many people think that boondocking is synonymous with the lack of hygiene and the contraction of viruses. With the way RVs have advanced to what they are today, this is the most ignorant of biases. The fact that you are far from other humans makes you at a lower risk of contracting a communicable disease. If anything, boondocking is healthy for more than one aspect of your being.

Also, just because you have a limited supply of water does not mean you will need to compromise on hygiene, so pack your cosmetics. Note that while out in the boonies, it is an adventure, not a fashion show.

Things to Fill Your Time

Take along pastimes like books and, if there is a group of you with children, pack a deck of cards, frisbees, and balls. If you are going to be close to a body of water, pack personal flotation devices (PFDs). Binoculars and a camera will enrich your experience.

Fishing rods should make the trip if fishing is allowed (do not forget to get a license). If you are lucky or good, you will be able to supplement your dinner. To give your outdoor experience some educational value, invest in a telescope for the nights and animal and vegetation manuals for during the day.

Folklore and historical literature of the region you are in will make for good reading at an after-dinner campfire. For those moments when it gets a little too quiet, take some headphones or perhaps a radio (that you will play softly). A guitar is not a bad idea. If you are going to play for people make sure that you know how to play, otherwise, it is all noise pollution.

Do a bit of writing, keep a journal or diary, and use the opportunity to straighten out your thoughts.

Comfort Items

A hammock and camping chairs are essential for outdoor leisure, and suntan lotion or sunblock is a necessity for hot weather. Do not forget those sunglasses, sunhats, bathing suits, and beach towels if you plan on working on your tan.

Chapter 8

Is America Boondock Friendly?

The word 'boondocking' with its current spelling and meaning is inherently American. Its association with RVs has become so tight as to be almost synonymous. You cannot boondock without an RV and, if you have a functional RV and you are not boondocking, then what are you doing with it? Boondocking is the true American outlook on the outdoors.

The general perception may change when RVs are spotted in towns and cities filling up water from non-designated spigots. Being parked up in some neighborhood trying to look inconspicuous is sometimes frowned upon.

Taking both schools of thought into consideration, what is the general American stance on boondocking?

A Migration of Sorts

In 2018, an estimated one million Americans were living in RVs permanently (Long, 2018). Today, the total number of RVs owned by families is 11.2 million. One in four of these families live in their RVs permanently (Go RVing, 2020).

That means that there are 2.8 million camper vans, trailers, and motorhomes out there that are permanent residences (theadventuretravelers.com, n.d.).

Some people do this for the adventure, while others do it for financial reasons. Whatever the motivations are, there is a visible growth in this change of lifestyle.

Size of the Market

The American outdoor industry is worth $459.8 billion, which was equal to 2.1% of the GDP in 2020. All 50 states contributed to this figure with the lowest contribution coming from Washington, D.C (1.1%). The states with the most revenue for the outdoor industry were Colorado, Utah, New Hampshire, Alaska, Wyoming, Maine, Montana, and the highest with a 5.2% contribution to the national GDP was Vermont.

Due to the lower costs associated with boondocking, more people are taking it up as a hobby. As opposed to flying out to a holiday destination and staying at a lodge or hotel, RVers have the benefit of sleeping in a rig that is also a means of transport. This arrangement works out cheaper than most forms of holiday making.

The attractive feature for many is freedom. People who are hands-on and adventurous tend to love this lifestyle. Since being cooped up in suburbia or the city is becoming increasingly unhealthy, many people are opting for nature's wildernesses where the area-to-person ratio is higher. As a testimony to this, 48 million families went camping in 2020. This figure is a substantial increase in the statistics for 2019 (Kampgrounds of America, 2021).

The projected turnout moving forward is about the same as in 2020.

Skilled professionals are taking up the lifestyle, too. The past year has taught industry monoliths that employees do not need to go into the office every day to get the job done. As such, there has been a spike in the growth of the tech-driven sector.

Graphic designers, writers, teachers, marketers, salesmen, call center agents, and many more only need their laptops and an Internet connection to work and earn money. Generation Y is experiencing a vast change in the corporate workspace. The capacity to work remotely comes with a lot of freedom. The majority of digital nomads are between 24 and 40 years of age.

This demographic makes up 38% of the RVing population (Widmer, 2019).

There is also a growing awareness of boondocking, and more so of the RVing lifestyle. The 10 million #vanlife posts on Instagram speak to this fact.

The U.S. RV industry contributes approximately $50 billion to the economy yearly (Widmer, 2019).

How Many Campsites Are There in America?

There are an estimated 16,000 campsites across America, 13,000 of which are privately owned, and 1,600 public or administered by the state (Widmer, 2019) Of these outdoor locations, 4,513 are RV parks (Hait, 2020).

When a campground calls itself an RV park, it implies that it has all the amenities a boondocker might need for an overnight stay (or longer). Things like shore power hookups, blackwater waste facilities, and spigots for topping up are all services such a resort will offer. However, national and provincial parks will be more inclined to offer the opportunity to boondock in the form of dispersed camping sites.

Five Favored States for Boondocking

As the statistics indicate, the boondocking culture is not limited to a select few locations, as this form of recreation is well-developed and the market is large. While it is fairly easy to find boondocking sites, you will be among many looking for these locations. As such, some locations are sought after, making it difficult to find isolation. These locations just become crowded as hundreds of RVers flock to the hotspots during the high season.

There are still many unknown and hidden locations. Only time and experience can help you find these gems and enjoy true serenity. For now, here are some of the best states with locations for boondocking.

Utah

Utah seems to be a favorite among RVers. Highway 163 and the Monument Valley offer multiple opportunities to pull over and stop.

Places for Boondocking in Utah

- Uinta-Wasatch-Cache National Forest. GPS coordinates: 41.833129, -111.598560.

    Uinta-Wasatch-Cache National Forest is 2.1 million acres of federally administered forest territory that is open to dispersed camping. This area encompasses the Wasatch Mountains where there are winter activities like snowboarding, skiing, and a version of the Oktoberfest in the summer. Salt Lake City, Ogden, Logan, and Park City are all proximal to the Wasatch Front.

    RVing in this area is of the dispersed kind with the normal government-enforced time limit of 30 days for both people and equipment.

    The rules specify your proximity to water: no less than 100 meters from any river, creek, lake, dam, or stream, and no further than 150 meters from the access road. Do not attempt to go off the beaten track. This means do not drive cross country, and when parking, stay close to the designated road. Not only is it prudent for boondockers to avoid marshy and wet areas but it is also prohibited by the rules of the area (USDA Forest Service, n.d.).

- Dixie National Forest. GPS coordinates: 37.677134, -112.677358.

    The total area of this designated forest is two million acres and it spans across southern Utah for about 170 miles. The elevation of the area is between 3,000 and 11,000 feet above sea level. Its climate can be extreme, ranging from 100 degrees Fahrenheit in the lower-lying areas to -30 on the higher elevations during the winter months. The picturesque cliffs guarding the Colorado River are definitely worth the trip (USDA Forest Service, 2021).

There are multiple boondocking opportunities in this area and they are free. However, you would need to get a permit from the nearest land office, which happens to be in Cedar City.

In this park, you must keep at least 200 meters away from the nearest watering hole and a maximum of 150 meters from the road or service track. Camping or parking is allowed for a maximum of 16 consecutive days at a time.

- Smithsonian Butte National Park, Via Back-Country Byway. GPS coordinates: 37.111188, -113.080829.

It is an area that is close to the towns of Grafton and Rockville. Take note that no camping is allowed in these two towns. The backcountry road is not suited to low clearance vehicles in wet weather. Truck campers with 4x4 capability can make it into this territory irrespective of driving conditions.

Note that parking is forbidden until you reach the top of the butte. This area is free of charge and seemingly unknown to the masses that flock to the adjoining Zion National Park (utah.com, 2021).

The Smithsonian Butte National Back-Country Byway area is also managed by the BLM and access is allowed all year long.

- Bryce Canyon National Park. GPS coordinates: 37.682415, -112.207449.

The Bryce Canyon National Park is known for its picturesque rock formations. It is situated in Southern Utah and covers an area of 35,800 acres. While the name refers to a single canyon, the national park contains a canyon complex. There is no need to go into the park itself to enjoy its beauty, as there are many places outside of it that offer locations for a picturesque boondocking experience (Nickels, 2020).

Traveling westward on Highway 12, you will find the E Fork Road or Forest Road (FR) 87 on your left, follow it. It is along this stretch that you will start seeing opportunities to pull over and set up a base (Nickels, 2020).

All the BLM rules apply, so try to use existing sites to minimize your impact on the ecology.

Arizona

Arizona is 72.69 million acres big, and 30.74 million of the state belongs to the national government. That makes 42.29% of Arizona's land area public property (ballotpedia.org, n.d.).

There is a lot of space for boondocking in the area and the climate makes it favorable. Make no mistake, the rest of RVing America knows this and you will see it in the numbers.

Places for Boondocking in Arizona

- KOFA National Wildlife Refuge. GPS Coordinates: 33.267683, -113.849335.

    This is a semi-arid area covering 670,000 of the Sonoran Desert, which has a complex and delicate ecology. There are rules in place that limit the impact of human presence on the surroundings. You are not allowed to camp or park within a quarter-mile of water (due to its limitations) and not more than 100 meters off the road. Like with all BLM domains, there is a 14-day limit to camping in this area.

- Scaddan Wash by the BLM. GPS coordinates: 33.661710, -114.146396.

    This particular place lies close to the crossroad desert town of Quartzite. The area is possibly the hottest place in the U.S. with its scalding summers and mild winters. There are more than 50 RV parks in the area. This place does not offer much in the line of privacy or isolation in the high seasons, but rather an RV festival-like atmosphere and camaraderie.

All BLM-managed sites in the area have a stay limit of 14 days per year and state-managed RV sites are either free or very cheap.

- Hackamore Road. GPS coordinates: 33.461237, -111.508665.

    Hackamore Road is known for its RVing. It is in the vicinity of Apache Junction, Canyon Lake, and the lost Dutchman Hiking Trail. The Superstition Mountains tower in the distance, surrounding Phoenix. They are a sight worth seeing at sunrise and sunset.

    This is also not the most remote area, but the advantage of the place is that there is cell phone coverage with most of the major networks (Nick The Rambling Man, 2020).

Wyoming

Wyoming is home to 64 million acres of unoccupied nature, with vast and many mountain ranges, endorheic basins, and the great plains. Its natural constitution makes it ideal for boondocking.

Places for Boondocking in Wyoming

- Lake Hattie. GPS coordinates: 47.2763, -95.1151.

    The camping spots around this lake area are dispersed and free. Spots close to the water can only accommodate smaller rigs. The maximum amount of stayover time permitted by the authorities is five days.

    If you are going to be driving a long distance to get here, you will drive in the general direction of Laramie.

The town is about 20 miles out and is the closest town to this location.

As you might imagine, there is a daytime buzz on the water, but the nights offer silence. The waterfront cannot accommodate larger rigs and thus these stay further back.

There is cell phone connectivity for the main telecommunications networks in the area.

- Upper Tetons. GPS coordinates: 43.7638, -110.5538.

If it is isolation you seek, this is where you will find it. The dispersed camping function of this location will give you the closest thing to boondocking you will ever get. The spot you want to be at is about a 20-minute drive from the Grand Teton National Park. The access road to this vantage point is rugged. Be mindful though, there have been reports of a surge in boondockers to all the favored sites (countrywide).

The area has cell phone coverage and is rated as generally neat and clean with average accessibility (freeroam.app, n.d.).

The high season is in summer with slightly fewer boondockers during spring and fall. If you want a chance at serenity in this area, winter would be the time. Look out for bears as they are known to frequent the area.

All the usual rules on environmental sustainability apply.

- Vedauwoo. GPS coordinates: 41.1544,-105.3745.

The Vedauwoo Glen Road, which is a tributary to I-80, will take you to the Vedauwoo Campsite. Being the boondocker that you are, you will be more interested in the opportunities that await if you carry on further down this road.

The area, as you will notice, is home to Pole Mountain, and if you are there during the spring, you may be lucky enough to see moose and elk in the distance.

The road that you are on becomes Forest Road 700 when you pass the Vedauwoo developed campsite. Many tracks branch off, but these may be hard on big rigs and vehicles with low clearances because the road surface is corrugated. It is along this stretch that you will start seeing opportunities to pull over and set up camp (Boondockers Bible, 2019).

The area is protected by rangers, but they are said to be lax, seeking out serious contraventions rather than just the minor oversights. Be that as it may, you know better and thus you should maintain your usual eco-friendly practices.

The best time to visit this area will be during the week rather than over weekends because then it becomes crowded and noisy (Boondockers Bible, 2019).

California

California is full of RVers and the hot desert climate can be credited for this. Dispersed camping is legal in areas managed by the BLM and these locations are ample.

One such area is the Death Valley National Park, which covers an area that is 3.4 million acres that reaches into Nevada. It is an area that is known for the Titus Canyon, colorful rocks, and rattlesnakes.

Places for Boondocking in California

- American Girl Mine. GPS coordinates: 32.85563, -114.78746.

As the name suggests, this location was originally a mine. It sits at the base of the Muchacho Mountains in Winterhaven, Imperial County. It was discovered by Johnson and Lohman in 1982 and under the shovel of many a miner rendered 30,000 tons of ore.

Those days are long gone, and the desert ecology of the area is protected by the BLM.

If warm weather is what you are after, then this is where you want to be. This particular area lies close to Arizona and Mexico, and 10miles out of Yuma. While the place is a known camping hotspot, its camping and RV spots are spread out, so it will not be as crowded as other popular RV venues. Be warned, motorheads with their OHVs love the spot too and may make it a bit noisy (Brady & Brady, n.d.).

The area around American Girl Mine offers dispersed camping. You will be bringing along everything you need and taking it back with you.

All BLM rules apply.

- Furnace Creek Road. GPS coordinates: 36.456457520497, -116.86789516884.

Furnace Creek is seven miles from Shoshone and 28 miles long. It lies within the unforgiving desert environment of the Death Valley National Park. Note that if you are going to camp anywhere in the confines of the park, you will not be allowed to drive off-road, make fires, or bring pets (National Park Service, 2021).

It's general location is near the border of Nevada and thus you can expect the same climate. As is characteristic of the Death Valley, Furnace Creek offers ample opportunity for exploring.

Permits are mandatory but easily attainable online. There is a fair number of dirt roads where camping is prohibited.

- Needles Point. GPS coordinates: 36.1235, -118.5185.

The name comes from the geological anomaly in the area. These are towering rock formations near the Kern River and about 10 miles north of Mountain Route 50.

Johnsondale, which is 20 miles away, is the nearest civilization to this location.

Your general direction will be in that of the Sequoia National Park. Once you get close to this conservation area, look for Forest Route 29s05. It will get you to some prime boondocking real estate.

Note that this area is remote without any cell phone reception, and therefore your safety protocols will have to be elevated to avoid mishaps that might immobilize you.

The area is under the administration of the National Park Service of the Canyonlands National Park.

Oregon

The state of Oregon has some prime locations for boondocking. The weather is temperate and the laws allow for dispersed camping on public land. The forests in the west offer a stark contrast to the mountains that define the eastern reaches of the state. There will be no shortage of scenery should you choose this as your boondocking location (RVshare, 2021).

Places for Boondocking in Oregon

- Hult Pond. GPS coordinates: 44.241184, -123.495426.

  This scenic area with the reservoir and surrounding wetland covers an area of 40 acres. It has a rich ecology, with a wide variety of animal and plant life. It is a prime spot for fishing, horse riding, and paddle boating, so you can pack your canoe (blm.gov, n.d.).

When driving from Eugene, Highway 99 and then 36 will get you from where you are to Lane County road No. 3640. The closest town to Hult Pond is Blachly, and the locals may not take kindly to being overrun by out-of-town RVers, so when you go there, try to behave. From here onwards, the BLM service roads will get you to your desired location. These roads are graded out of dirt and will make you work to earn your reward (outdoorsy.com, n.d.).

The area is managed by the BLM, and all of the standard rules apply.

- Burnt Ranch Road. GPS coordinates: 44.6129, -120.2105.

Access to this area depends on the time of year as snow levels can make it impassable. This area is away from civilization and does not have any cell phone reception. Traveling this route will take you through the general vicinity of the John Day Fossil Beds National Monument. The closest town to it is Mitchel, which is five miles away. If you follow the Ochoco Road, it will bring you to your destination (BLM John Day River—Lower Burnt Ranch, n.d.).

This area falls under the administration of the BLM. Once you get off the highways, you will be on rugged roads that will be tougher on trailers and vehicles with low clearances. There is no signage for directions so it can become tricky for vehicle and trailer combinations exceeding 30 feet.

The areas you will be looking for are rustic and dispersed, and so you will be responsible for everything you need.

- Sage Hen Hill Road. GPS coordinates: 43.5818, -119.3081.

In your search for this tranquility, your journey will take you to Central Oregon. You will be heading into the southern part of Harney County, which is 73 miles from Lakeview. The Sage Hen Hill Wilderness Study Area is another location that defines boondocking.

The total amount of public land covered by the Sage Hen Hill Wilderness is 8,520 acres of rolling low hills. There is no cellphone reception and a lot of space with dirt roads being the only access (Valtzis, n.d.).

This area is 600 feet above sea level and consists of semi-arid hills covered in sagebrush. It also has a hiking trail.

The standard BLM rules apply.

Part 2

Powering Your RV

Chapter 1

Minimum Electrical Requirements

One of the salient characteristics of an RV is its capability to run electronically powered appliances. In order for this to happen, there is a complex network of wiring, switches, fuses, and electrical sources onboard. Through time, these systems have been improved upon and standardized, making every RV's basic electrical setup more or less the same.

The Ability to Store Power

For the RV to function as a stand-alone unit, it must renew its electrical reserves regularly. Additionally, the recreational vehicle's ability to replenish its power should be multi-faceted.

Hookup Leads

The first requisite of an RV is its ability to hook up to an external electrical source. This capability is often seen at work in RV parks where there are posts next to parking spaces with plug sockets. Most times, there are two receptacles that are different in appearance. This is not usually a brain teaser as the plug on the lead that extends from your RV fits one socket properly, and the other not at all.

Aside from the physical adaptability, these sockets also determine something else that is more important, namely, the amount of electrical current. These sockets in amps represent 30-amp and 50-amp options.

Most RVs have their electrical hookup cable permanently fastened to the RV. The shore power cable, as it is commonly known, is responsible for bringing power into the RV. Then the electrical appliances inside the rig can operate and the onboard power storage banks (or coach battery array) can recharge.

The Two Kinds of Kinds of Electrical Service

The logic employed here is: Smaller RVs need less. The lesser rig only has one air conditioner (if any) and cannot be operated simultaneously with too many other appliances. Assuming the fridge is on at the same time, along with the coach battery charger, there is not much else in the line of appliances that can be used without causing problems.

Some campsites only have 50-amp sockets, but this can easily be remedied with the use of adapters. These adapters are sold at outdoor adventure stores.

RVs with a 50-amp capability tend to be larger and capable of bearing more electrical appliances. These RVs can be the size of a bus and can support two air conditioners, a home entertainment system, washing machines, and a large fridge, and this is all thanks to a faster flow of current.

Power Storage Capacity

Batteries provide the RV with the ability to store electricity from the electrical pedestal. Aside from the starter battery, there should be at least four deep-cycle batteries connected in parallel. These should be 12 volts each, creating a battery bank capable of delivering a sustained supply of power to the RV. These batteries will not provide all aspects of power to the RV, but they can be depended on to sustain the necessities. With the help of an inverter, this setup is also capable of generating power for the AC outlets.

Maintaining Battery Life

The first and most energy-efficient way of recharging your batteries is when driving. The alternator in the engine compartment recharges the battery when the motor is running. When the starter battery is fully replenished, the alternator still generates power for all the other electronic facets of a vehicle. In an RV, the coach batteries are set up to use the current coming off the alternator to keep its reserves topped up.

While plugged into shore power, not only do you have the ability to use electrical appliances more liberally but the current coming from the external source puts life back into the batteries.

When parked out in the boonies for an extended period, you are prone to run out of power. This is the reason why many motorhomes come standard with a generator. While operating, the generator can charge the batteries and supply AC power needs.

Generators use fuel like gasoline or diesel and can be expensive to run. The answer to this dilemma comes in the form of renewable energy sources. In the case of RVs, these are solar panels and wind turbines. The latter is clean and cheap, and once installed they do not need anything other than nature to generate power. While the aforementioned sources may produce results slower than conventional methods, they still make a substantial contribution to your power reserves.

The Capacity to Be Electronically Independent

The batteries are the basis of an RVs electronic independence. Their capacity to deliver a consistent current over a prolonged space of time can be extended by adding more batteries in parallel. This does not necessarily allow you to run more devices but rather the same appliances for longer.

The average battery's life cannot be allowed to drop below 50% and thus, no matter where you are, you should be able to charge them up before their power capacity falls too low.

Generators

Depending on the power-producing capacity of a generator, these machines are capable of replenishing a battery's life while simultaneously feeding current to AC drawing appliances.

Alternate Current Source

This is crucial for heavy-duty appliances like refrigerators, air conditioners, microwaves, and whatever you decide to plug into the AC wall sockets. When operating autonomously, the RV is capable of creating its own AC via means of the generator or an inverter.

Direct Current Source

The direct current of an RV is provided by the batteries and is important for fans, lights, water pumps, furnace motors, and inverters.

The Ability to Convert Between AC and DC

Not all appliances use AC, and likewise not all use DC. Things like fridges have been engineered to run off either AC, propane, and, in some cases, DC. This is called a three-way fridge. Not all appliances have this flexibility and thus can only work on a certain type of current. Thankfully, there are ways to convert between the two types of power.

Fridges, air conditioners, and microwaves rely on the use of an inverter to turn the DC from a battery into AC. Inverters seldom come as a standard feature on an RV.

When plugged into shore power or dependent on a generator, DC appliances can only use the inbound power once it has been converted. The converter, which is normally near the coach battery array (or part of a hybrid inverter) converts the 120 volts of AC to a 12 volts of DC, which then recharges the batteries. The batteries then feed the DC requirements of the RV.

A Capacity to Self-Regulate

The coach batteries need to be monitored. Overcharging or draining below a certain level may damage these batteries and hence they need to be watched.

Selecting Power Sources

Two of the main AC power sources available are shore power and generator power. Both lead to the circuit board. Any RV electrical system can only use one AC input at a time. The standard RV gets its alternating current from one of two places: the grid (shore power) or the generator. A device called an automatic transfer switch is what selects between the two.

The safety aspect gives priority to one option, which in the case of an RV, is the generator. This means that should there be a situation where the generator gets triggered while the shore power is live, the switch crosses over and connects the generator while cutting off the shore power supply, and in so doing averts a dangerous AC overload.

Battery Monitoring

Power from an RV's coach battery array is the lifeblood of any rig. Your ability to stay aware of its status is important. Should a battery's life deplete to a state below 50%, its overall lifespan will shorten, so this is especially true if the battery is drained regularly. Battery monitoring in tandem with the relevant knowledge is vital to preventing damage, maintaining a steady power supply, and ensuring that they last as long as possible.

Fuses

A fuse box is the equivalent of circuit breakers on a distribution board. While circuit breakers service AC (the type of electricity that comes from the pedestal), a fuse box manages DC, which originates from batteries. A standard RV has two fuse boxes, one is for electronics associated with the vehicle's ability to drive, and the other is the accommodational functionality of the RV.

Circuit Breakers

These are important for preserving infrastructure and preventing unnecessary damage when the inbound current becomes too much or unstable. Its defense mechanism against electrical disaster is to break the flow of current by switching off. It will keep switching off for as long as the fault persists. It may be inconvenient at the time, but it prevents cables and appliances from burning out.

Once battery power is changed by an inverter, it becomes AC. As such, it is then controlled by the circuit breaker.

Chapter 2

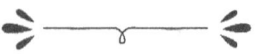

Understanding Your Electrical System

While the basic electrical elements of an RV may be the same, there are many different versions of these setups. The market that supplies these gadgets is ever-growing, demanding better innovations to make the RV more efficient.

The Three Divisions of an RVs Electrical System

The principles that govern the power supply of these rigs are very much the same: All RVs consist of three electrical systems that depend on each other.

The Automotive System

The automotive system is centered around the single 12-volt battery that kicks the engine to life every time you turn the ignition. This battery is, in turn, dependent on the alternator to keep it charged. Between the alternator and the starter battery, all the electronic requirements of the vehicular parts of an RV are met. These parts include all navigation lights on the outside, the horn, sensors, alarm systems, instrument panels, electric windows, satellite navigation, radios, etc.

The battery itself is high performance in that it is capable of giving a large spike of current that is enough to start the engine. Unlike a deep-cycle battery, it is unable to give a sustained performance and is likely to die relatively fast, and thus it depends on the alternator for sustenance. Throughout the drive, the starter battery feeds the electrical needs of the vehicle.

The alternator, which is initially triggered with the motor at the turning of the ignition, gets a marginal amount of power from the battery at the starting of the engine. It turns that power into a much stronger current and supplies the battery and other DC requirements on the vehicle.

In the case of an RV, the alternator is hooked up to the house battery bank and charges it while the engine is running. Furthermore, additional settings allow for the onboard fridge to work while the vehicle is in motion.

The alternator gives off AC. Without a means for conversion, AC and DC are incompatible. For this reason, there is a set of diodes that are connected to the alternator, and they cancel out the alternating quality of the current generated by the alternator. The resulting current is DC, which is then compatible with starter and coach batteries and all electrical aspects needing DC.

In short, the automotive system is centered around a collaboration between a 12-volt battery and an alternator. These are mainly responsible for the automotive aspects of the rig but are also capable of charging coach batteries.

The DC Coach System

The DC coach system is defined by a combination of more than one 12-volt battery. These batteries are connected in parallel to keep the voltage the same. An outstanding feature of this setup is its capacity to be charged regularly and deliver a steady stream of direct current over a longer period.

Unlike the automotive battery, the coach variant is required to give longevity rather than power or intensity. The more batteries you add in parallel, the longer you will be able to draw power from said bank. The downside of the latter is that the bank would then take longer to charge.

These batteries can be charged from the alternator when the vehicle is running and from other sources like solar power, electrical pedestals, and generators. The incoming power from generators and the grid passes through a converter before it reaches the battery.

Everything in an RV uses DC with an exception for the fridge, microwave, air conditioner, and devices that plug into the AC outlets. With the assistance of an inverter, the battery bank can power AC drawing appliances.

The DC coach system is the essence of an RVs capacity to function autonomously.

The AC Coach System

The AC coach system is 120 volts strong. It is lower than the standard strength, but the same type of current that is available to a domestic setting. AC generally gets used for heavy-duty appliances and, in this case, is a lot more powerful than the DC currents on RVs. In the rig, this type of current feeds the air conditioner, refrigerator, and microwave. The 120 volts make their way through a circuit breaker board to the plug sockets and the relevant appliances in the RV.

What is left of the power goes to the batteries via a converter that dilutes the current into a conductible form. The converter then sends it to the cells at a manageable voltage of DC.

AC power comes through the pedestals at RV parks. Once they are plugged in, they can fulfill any electrical need on the RV, but not all at the same time. The 3,600-watt cap on a 30-amp connection should never be exceeded. To stay within these parameters, one would normally avoid running the air conditioner if the fridge is connected to power. The combination of the two comfortably fits into the 3,600-watt pool, but then it would marginalize the other appliances that can be used.

On an RV there are two sources of AC. The first one is the generator, which serves the purpose of charging up the coach batteries in an off-the-grid setting. It is as effective as the electrical pedestal at the RV park (the second source), but cannot be operated for extended periods. Generators also have an impact on the natural setting (noise pollution) and the fuel limitations when out in the sticks.

Electrical Pedestals' Service in Amps

Your RV falls into one of two categories based on its electrical needs.

30 Amps

Thirty-amp electrical services are installed on RVs that do not have big power requirements. These make up the majority of RVs. The 30-amp receptacle has a 120-volt hot-wire slot on the left, a neutral on the right, and a slot reserved for the ground or earthing at the top (in the event of a leak). A 30-amp service translates into 3,600 watts and this is the power available to the RV's electrical system.

If your RV is running a 30-amp service, its standard power needs will correspond with its electrical capabilities.

50 Amps

As mentioned before, a 50-amp service is the kind of service that occurs on larger vehicles. A tell-tale sign of a vehicle with a 50-amp service is its two air conditioners. The 50-amp plug is also unique in that it has four prongs. On the receptacle (plug socket), the neutral occurs in the center bottom and a ground on the top center with the hot-wire slots on the left and right. This is often referred to as a 120/240 split phase service.

The split phase indicates the electrical current to the RV is being split and this then makes it capable of 12,000 watts, which is almost four times more powerful than a 30-amp service.

Watts, Amps, and Volts

Watts, amps, and volts are universal measures for electrical attributes. They can be found depicting the capabilities of electrical appliances and sources (like plug sockets and batteries). They are vitally important standards that define compatibility among devices.

Volts

A volt is the force with which a current flows. This is measured in units of current against units of resistance (in Ohms). Knowing the amount of voltage required is critical to the understanding of how your RV works.

Amp and Watts

The word "Amp" refers to a unit of electrical current (a Coulomb) that flows past a point in the conductor during one second. In the case of your RV, you are getting either 30 or 50 amps.

To calculate your power requirements, you will need to convert the current measurement from amps to watts. If your service is 30 amps and your voltage 120, then you multiply the amps by the voltage (30 x 120), and the answer you get will be in watts (3,600 watts).

The 50-amp service has 240 volts split in half at the pedestal and distributed in the same configuration to the RV. In the RV, there is a distribution board with two mains, each supplying 120 volts. To work out how much power you have at your disposal, you multiply the total voltage by the amps (240 x 50). The resulting current will be 12,000 watts. Should one of the mains not work or remain off, your RV will only have access to 6,000 watts.

Watts refers to the rate of one Joule of energy used or produced per second. By mathematically converting your power pool into watts, you will be able to calculate your power needs and compare them to your power supply. For example, the average RV fridge uses 600 watts, and this means it consumes 600 Joules of energy per second. The 30-amp RV receives 3,600 Joules of energy per second. When you are running your fridge, you deduct 600 watts from that pool of energy, and this then leaves you with a balance of 3,000 watts.

All lights, timers, detectors, and appliances, big or small, draw from this pool, so when calculating your electrical needs, everything needs to be factored in. Should you attempt to use more than you have at your disposal, your RV will shed devices, meaning it will stop sending current to certain devices and they will switch off. Overloading power sources sometimes damages appliances.

There are stickers at the backs or bottoms of appliances that indicate the amps, voltage, or watts of a device. This information and a bit of math will help you accurately determine your vehicles' capacity to supply your appliances with power.

How It Works

The automotive DC system transfers direct current to the coach system's batteries when the vehicle's engine is running. If the engine runs for long enough, the coach system's batteries will be topped off. To prevent overcharging the power from the alternator to the battery bank may be manipulated so that it stops sending power when the batteries are full.

While the automotive system can charge the coach system, the opposite is not possible through the standard setup. When the engine of the vehicle is off, the automated system is completely isolated from both AC and DC coach systems.

The DC coach system is connected to an array of 12-volt batteries. These batteries, no matter how many, must always be connected in parallel. The reason is so that the power coming out of them is never more than 12 volts. Should batteries be placed in series, the DC coach systems voltage will be increased and result in blown fuses and possibly damaged electronics.

These batteries feed many DC components of the RV, and they are also a source of AC power to the RV via the means of an inverter.

The coach system is charged by shore power (grid power) using the correct amp service, which is either 30 amps or 50 amps, or a generator. Both these sources produce AC power, but a mechanism called a converter changes the current to a 12-volt DC charge and this is then capable of replenishing the coach's batteries.

The DC coach system has a fuse box that serves as a gatekeeper for inbound DC. Should the current exceed 12 volts, the relevant fuses will all burn and in so doing discontinue the flow of current.

AC voltage is prevalent in homes and industry, favored for its capacity to bear higher voltages to bigger electrical demands, hence its capacity to run heavy-duty machinery.

The AC coach system on an RV is set to 120 volts, and this is 10 times more than that of the related DC system and justifiably so. Aside from running the bigger appliances on board, it also feeds the batteries.

There are plug sockets throughout the RV that depend on the 120-volt AC.

Generators are also capable of delivering AC at 120 volts. These are normally used when far from shore power.

The AC version of an overload gatekeeper is the circuit breaker. Should there be an overload or leak, the circuit breaker for the relevant line will switch off, disconnecting the current.

Chapter 3

Inverters

Due to the availability of two types of electricity, it is necessary to have a mechanism capable of converting power, especially since AC power cannot be stored. The role of the inverters among the electronic demands of modern society is essential.

When AC is produced by the grid and generators, it is either a product of fossil fuels or a conversion from another kind of energy. Generators in a non-industrial setting like RVing tend to be noisy and are generally eco-unfriendly. For this reason, they are only kept as a power source for batteries. Since batteries are capable of storing power, they are convenient for off-the-grid purposes.

The shortfall of a battery is that it cannot power certain utilities and thus the need for an inverter. The inverter changes the DC, which only travels in one direction along a circuit, into an alternating bidirectional current. The amount of AC power that comes through an inverter depends on its intake from the battery and its capability to produce AC.

Inverters cannot produce electricity by themselves as they rely on DC for a power source.

How Inverters Work

Inverters range from complex to rudimentary, manipulating battery power to mimic that of AC.

Battery Current

The positive terminal of an electrical cell (battery) emits electrons that vie to achieve equilibrium. The only way that these electrons can achieve this is by flowing back into the cell via the negative pole. For this to happen, the circuit needs to be complete. Electrons create energy as they flow along conductors and through devices, powering the devices. This flow of current operates in a steady stream and single direction, hence the name, direct current.

The Inverter Mechanism

The main components of an inverter are the array of switches known as insulated gate bipolar transistors (IGBTs). These work in tandem with a device called a controller.

As stated in the name, IGBTs are switches that, when closed, form current-conducting circuits. There is more than one circuit connected to the incoming stream in two different ways. When one circuit is closed, the current flows clockwise. When the latter is open and the other closed, the current flows counterclockwise.

The device used to monitor the quality of an inverter's output is called an oscilloscope. On these oscilloscopes, it becomes apparent that there are three different qualities of AC. The monitoring device displays these qualities as waves of equal sizes on either side of a horizontal line.

The most basic form of AC will show square waves of equal sizes alternating on the negative and positive sides of the zero-voltage line (the horizontal line). Though these square waves are not per se representative of waves, they depict the alternating nature of the current.

The inverter alone is not capable of sufficiently powering AC appliances and thus needs to be modified. To create a better quality of current, more components (IGBTs) are added to the inverter. These create a higher level of sophistication and are thus projected on the oscilloscope as a square wave with extra steps. This is known as a modified sine wave. The kind of inverter that uses this principle produces a current that works on more appliances but is still a step down from real AC.

The next step in pure sine development are waves that are projected as clean oscillations with smooth and flowing curves crossing zero voltage lines without lingering. The process of refinement within the inverter becomes even more complex and the controller employed is capable of modulating the activity of many more IGBTs.

Once the latter is achieved, the AC emitted from the inverter is clean, constant, and of high quality. All AC drawing appliances can operate on this power and do so efficiently. The type of inverter that produces this kind of AC is a pure sine inverter.

Stepping Up the Power

The inverted current produced is not enough to meet the demands placed on it by the RV's system. For this reason, every standalone inverter comes with a built-in transformer. It is not a given that you will get the shore supply of 3,600 watts from every inverter, so this means that you will have to calculate your power needs before buying one.

Sine Waves

As explained above, not all inverters are equal. Each inverter is defined by the quality of the sine waves they produce. There are three different types of sine wave inverters.

Square Sine Wave Inverters

Square sine wave inverters are the most basic of all. These inverters are the cheapest and can only support motors, this makes them incompatible with the RV electrical system.

Modified Sine Wave Inverters

These inverters are a compromise on the pure sine wave variant and thus work out cheaper. Whether or not it is advisable to buy them depends on what you are planning.

On a modified sine wave inverter audio devices will give off a hum, fluorescent lights are not as bright and refrigerators will not work as efficiently.

However, if you just want to run a TV, certain tools, a microwave, a griddle, and perhaps an electric kettle, the quality AC rendered by a modified sine wave inverter will suffice.

The main symptoms of devices not being compatible with these kinds of inverters are unusual noise and overheating.

Pure Sine Wave Inverters

The inner workings of these items are complex in comparison to their modified counterparts. The best form of AC is the type that comes from the grid. This kind of current is represented on the oscilloscope by pure curvature as voltage rises to its optimum positive point and drops again crossing the zero voltage line (which also represents the change in the flow of a current's direction) and moves towards the negative optimum voltage.

Provided that the power needs of appliances are the same as what comes out of the wall socket, any AC device can be used with the electrical service provided by the pure sine wave inverter.

Hybrid Inverters

An outstanding feature of the hybrid inverter is its ability to synchronize with grid power. It is capable of combining converter and inverter into a single unit. The standard inverter cannot work in tandem with an ongoing shore power supply. It often uses a three-way switch to select the priority source of AC.

The hybrid is capable of topping up on the demands of the RV if the grid source is found wanting. This is particularly so when there is only a 15- or 20-amp shore power source available.

Should the power demand dissipate to a manageable load, the inverse function then initiates. The hybrid inverter will stop using power from the battery, take on current from the shore supply, convert it to DC, and start charging the batteries.

How to Choose an Inverter for Your RV

The first decision to make is whether you are going to spend a bit more and get the pure sine wave version, or spend less on the modified inverter and more money on replacing the damaged appliances. In the long run, the modified inverter will turn out to be more expensive after all.

Another downside of choosing the cheaper variant is that it is less efficient, and this means that the appliances may use more power in that they take longer to work and deplete the coach batteries. The batteries will need to be charged more often, which may take a toll on the fuel costs associated with the generator. Eventually, because of the repeated charging, the overall lifespan of the generator and the batteries will shorten.

This is another long-term loss associated with modified sine wave batteries, making them a costlier option than a pure sine wave inverter.

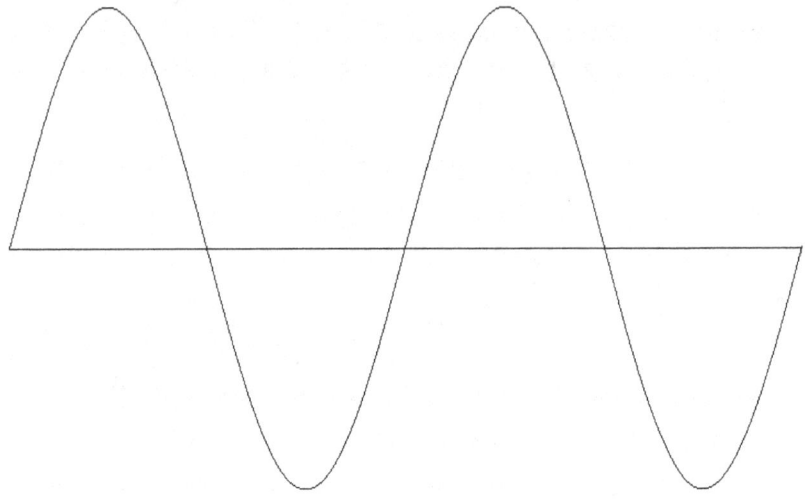

What Are Your Power Needs?

Just because shore power allows you 3,600 watts, it does not mean that you need the same in an inverter. By calculating AC-reliant items that are likely to operate simultaneously, you will receive an indication of how much you are likely to need (in watts). If you feel that your power requirements are a bit high, you can try swapping older model appliances for later releases. Modern-day appliance manufacturers are making it a priority to build energy-efficient devices.

The bigger your RV, the more power you will need, especially because the size of your rig is proportional to the number of people the rig will be accommodating.

The popular inverters are capable of 1,500 watts to 2,000 watts. If you have a rig that is medium or large, and you have not found ways to swap out some of your electrical needs for other energy sources, you will need to install an inverter of a substantial capability. Additionally, if you are going to be occupying your RV with your significant other and perhaps a child, economical living will become a lot more difficult. At this point, you may want to consider an inverter with a capacity of anywhere between 2,000 watts and 3,000 watts.

Accommodating the Current Setup While Planning for the Future

What is the size of your battery bank? The size can play a role in what inverter you install. If you have a low capacity to store the power, you are not likely to use a lot of electricity as you will apply it to the bare necessities only. This likely means you do not intend on using a lot of AC. If this is the case, you will go for an inverter with a small DC converting capacity.

On the other hand, if you have a complex array of appliances, hookups, a generator, and a solar array, then you will be looking for a sophisticated inverter, perhaps something that can easily simplify your electrical setup while possessing a capacity to deliver a larger AC. If you need more AC, then you may be in the market for a hybrid inverter, which costs a bit more, but is still effective.

From Battery to Inverter

The first rule of connecting your inverter is to situate it as close to your batteries as possible. The reason why you want to do this is to minimize attenuation (voltage loss).

Another factor that affects your flow of current is the width of the cable you use: the thicker the cable, the lower the voltage loss. Note that the lower the cable gauge (numerically), the thicker the actual cable. The unit of measurement for cables is the American wiring gauge (AWG).

There are many options available on the market and thus choosing cables can be confusing. The battery jumper cord and welding cable work just fine for the job and are sold in different sizes. Note that welding cable tends to be expensive, so unless you have one lying around, it is best to buy and modify jumper cables. The inverter should be connected directly to the battery with the wires on the corresponding poles (positive to positive and negative to negative).

Inverter to RV

The connections to the AC/outlet side of an inverter are not as simple. There are different methods for doing it.

Method A

The best way of connecting your inverter is also the most complicated. Here you will run the outlet cables from the inverter to a transfer switch and then to the distribution box inside the RV. The reason for the transfer switch is so that you only permit AC from one source at a time, thus averting an overload.

By now, you realize that the inverter is powered by the coach batteries. The batteries are, in turn, powered by AC power through a converter, so it is necessary to put in place measures that prevent the AC coming out of the inverter from going through the converter. That will create a loop that will waste voltage and drain the batteries quickly. You can prevent this by splitting the distribution board inside the RV and placing a switch on the same side of the DB as the shore power.

Another method is to place a cut-off switch between the AC supply and converter, which you will turn off when the inverter is working.

Method B

A less elaborate way of routing inverter power is by using an extension lead. Plug it into the AC part of an inverter, thread it through an open space or a window, and then plug it into a multi-plug adapter. Needless to say, this is not the neatest solution.

Method C

What some RVers do to keep the process simple is connect the inverter to one plug socket. This outlet is then dedicated to the inverter and will not work when the RV is connected to shore power. The single outlet inverter method creates the risk of overload, especially when multi-plug adapters are used on it.

Method D

This method is more industrious than, yet not as effective as, Method A. Here, you will connect a lead to the AC side of the inverter and route to a spot close to your shore power cable. You will then connect it to a receptacle that fits your shore power cable, and make it a permanent fixture on the external RV wall.

When you are not plugged into shore power, you can then plug into the aforementioned socket for inverter-generated AC power. With this method, you need not worry about an ATS, but you will need a cut-off to your converter to avoid the previously mentioned power loop scenario.

Additionally, this method would require that you unplug from the modification and turn off your cut-off switch when you run your generator. The main reason for this is the generator would not be able to charge your battery bank with the cut-off engaged.

When the generator runs, it feeds AC power to all the respective outlets and devices in the RV.

Chapter 4

Generators

In its application to RVing, generators serve to charge batteries and feed specific power needs within the RV. In certain rigs, there is a selector switch that gives generators priority over incoming shore power. So if you engage the generator while the RV is connected to shore power, the aforementioned switch will disconnect the current flowing from the grid and give precedence to the generator.

Why Do RVs Need a Generator?

A generator runs off fuel (often out of the fuel tank of a vehicle) and distributes power through the converter to the batteries to charge them. While it runs, it also feeds AC to specific devices onboard the RV. A generator is the ultimate source of off-grid energy for an RV. Unlike an alternator, solar power, and shore power, its operation is independent and can deliver power at any time. The characteristics of a generator make it indispensable when dry camping in an RV.

Onboard Generators

The upside of having an onboard generator is that you do not need to go outside to operate it. This means no trips in and out of the RV to toggle the switch on a rainy or snowy day. The standard generator on an RV is custom-designed to handle the AC load of the rig while charging its batteries.

Onboard generators tend to be quite noisy and cause vibrations throughout the whole RV when they are working. From an environmental perspective, this is a good incentive to run them as little as possible.

Portable Generators

A key factor of the portable generator is its size. It is easy to store and thus makes a good backup for RVs with pre-existing generators. Boondockers normally tote these along as a contingency plan.

The benefit of the portable generator is that you can place it away from the RV when it is in operation. Doing this is beneficial in that the fumes from the machine are far from you and hence the chances of you inhaling the carbon monoxide are much slimmer.

How to Choose a Generator

The two main things you look for in a generator are its ability to last and its compatibility with your needs. What amount of watts do you need to fulfill your RV's needs? Just because you have a 30-amp service in your RV, it does not mean that you will need 3,600 watts of energy. When choosing your generator, you will take into account the most electricity you are likely to use at the same time. After doing your calculations, the answer to this question will help you decide what generator to buy.

Make sure that the generator you plan on buying has the correct fittings, receptacles, and enough of them. Normally, all you will need is a receptacle on it that is compatible with your shore cable.

Since you cannot watch it all the time and as a human you are prone to forget, the generator you buy will need to have safety mechanisms. The best and most common safety mechanism is the automatic cut-out switch. This switch kicks in when the generator's oil is low or if there are other anomalies detected by the generator. Some of these machines have a carbon monoxide sensor. When it detects an abnormal buildup of the toxic gas, the sensors trigger the cut-off switch.

Noise Control

The amount of noise a generator produces when operational should be influential to your decision. You will mostly use your generator when in the boonies and a purely natural environment. The racket coming from a noisy 4-stroke engine will kill the mood and likely draw unwanted attention.

The noise emitted from generators is multi-faceted: The engine's firing reverberates through the oil pan at the bottom of the machine, creating a metallic ring along with its sputtering noises. Furthermore, the engine noises are pumped through the exhaust outlet and escape through the air intake. If the generator is on a solid surface, it is likely to create vibrations in the surrounding structure, and thus if you have an onboard generator, its presence when operating can be jarring.

You will notice that the more a generator ages, the noisier it gets. This increase in sound emission is due to mounting washers wearing out and nuts and bolts loosening. These cause rattling. Even one loose mounting can increase the noise from a generator exponentially. When servicing yours, make sure that all the screws are tightened and check mountings, nuts, clamps, and fittings for any kind of looseness.

If you have an onboard version, the same process is required. The outer casing should not be secured directly to the RV's panels without elastomeric mountings. These mountings are combinations of different metals and rubber that have insulating qualities that absorb shock or vibration.

The use of these will reduce noise from the generator and any vibrations caused within the RV. Aftermarket absorptive padding on the walls of the generator compartment will muffle the noise. This padding is available in options like acoustic foam, soundproof paint, and more.

There are ways to minimize the noise using rejected materials. Egg cartons, cardboard, and old rugs will work as well for sound suppression. The trick is to cut the material of your choice to size and stick it to the inner walls of the generator's compartment. Be sure that you do not block any vents as this will cause problems like overheating.

Portable generators tend to be a lot smaller and emit less noise. Be that as it may, they can still disturb the peace while outside. You can reduce the environmental impact of a generator by placing it on a soft surface, replacing its muffler with a bigger, better one, and better yet, you could build a canopy for it out of noise absorbent material.

Fuel Sources

If your generator is built-in and a standard feature of the RV, then it will feed straight out of your fuel tank, thus using diesel or gasoline.

Diesel Generators

Those that are installed on trailers will be inclined to use gasoline or propane as is the case with portable versions.

Diesel generators are not as common. While this type of generator is easier to maintain and generally has a longer life span, it emits a lot more pollutants into the atmosphere. They are prevalent as onboard fixtures among RVs with diesel engines.

Gasoline Generators

Gasoline, which is the most common fuel type for generators, is also the most problematic. When a gasoline generator stands for too long, the gas in a tank degrades, oxidizing and eventually clogging up pipes. In extreme scenarios, the machine becomes inefficient if not inoperable. There are aftermarket fuel stabilizing products that slow down these processes. The safest course of action is to drain out the fuel when the generator is not in use.

Propane Generators

Propane presents fewer problems and is more environmentally friendly. Its carbon monoxide output is almost half that of gasoline and 2% of that emitted by its diesel counterparts (Canadian propane Association, n.d.).

It is easier to store with no risk of spillage and is well preserved in its pressurized canister. The canister maintains the propane's integrity over long periods of time.

While it is healthier for the environment, propane tends to be less efficient than gasoline, burning faster while costing more.

Dual Fuel Generators

Some generators are capable of using two different types of fuel. These combinations are commonly available in propane and gasoline. The main advantage of using a dual fuel generator is variety. This is something you will opt for if you do not want to be limited to one energy source.

Power Outputs/Requirements

The kind of generator you use will depend on your power needs. Ultimately, the amount of power (in watts) vs. the amount a generator can deliver will determine what kind of generator will work for you.

The average RV will need a generator that is capable of between 2,000 watts and 4,000 watts. Your energy production will not be the same as shore power when using a generator. The reason for this is because of the cost associated with buying and running bigger generators and the generator's tendency to give off less current when running for a prolonged amount of time.

Manufacturers place the startup power value of a generator on the labeling and not the running power. This is an important factor as the starting power is not what you will have at your disposal to run appliances over an extended time. A generator's wattage spikes for the first few seconds of engagement and then drops to a lower average production rate.

Knowing this, perhaps it is then prudent to deduct 25% off the advertised wattage before factoring in your needs.

Safe Operation

Ventilation is of the utmost importance when running a generator. These machines give off fumes and when kept in an enclosed area will build up of carbon monoxide. The effects on a human in the same space as the said apparatus could be fatal.

There will never be any reason for you to plug your generator into a shore power receptacle, so do not do it.

Generators create electricity so all hazards associated with an electrical supply apply to it, including shock. Make sure that you do not become a conductor when handling a live generator by wearing shoes and keeping your hands dry.

Avoid operating a generator in wet weather. If you have to, protect it with a waterproof covering that is suspended above the machine. Never cover a generator with a tarp, plastic, or similar material while in operation. A better idea is to build a waterproof noise suppressant cover.

Being predominantly metal, the components of a generator make perfect heat conductors. For this reason, kids and animals, and even adults are in danger of getting burned should they touch it in the wrong place.

Maintenance

The generator is a simplified version of an engine, but with that said, it is still sophisticated. Be that as it may, as an owner, you do not need a professional skill-set to own or maintain one.

Cleanliness

Like with every other item in your possession, an important part of maintenance is keeping all items clean. The buildup of grease and dirt can expedite wear and aging. A soapy cloth, degreaser, and pressurized air are all good ways to clean generators. Pressurized water hoses cause more damage than good and should thus be avoided.

Oil Maintenance

Like every engine, the generator needs fuel to work. If the fuel runs out, the engine will switch off, but should the oil run dry while the motor is running it will seize up, meaning it will never work again.

Some generators have built-in, low-oil warnings alerts or automatic cut-outs. Others only have a dipstick. It is vitally important to the health of your generator not only to make sure that there is enough oil but to change it regularly.

If your oil changes color over a short period, or perhaps you find that you have to refill it regularly, your generator may need servicing. Another reason why you could be losing oil is because of leaks.

Drain Fuel Before Storing

As mentioned before, gasoline generators need to be drained before going into storage to avoid deterioration. Diesel engines and tanks are not as problematic, but it would not hurt to get into the habit anyways. The drained fuel need not be discarded and can be kept in safe and appropriate storage until needed again.

Check Filters Regularly

Air filters may need to be cleaned after every trip and be replaced once a month (Gabrielse, 2015). Bear in mind that dirty filters can cause heavier fuel consumption. Look into those fuel filters, too: A build-up of impurities can impede a generator's performance.

Check on Screws, Clamps, and Mountings

Generators create vibrations that cause rattles over time due to screws and mountings becoming loose. Look out for worn rubber washers that need to be replaced and be sure that the required screws, nuts, and bolts are all present. Check hose clamps for integrity as faulty or loose clamps may lead to excessive fuel loss.

Service Your Generator Annually

The maximum amount of time that should be allowed to transpire between services is one year. The more you use a generator, the more often you will need to service it. If in your own capacity you care for it properly, you will be abreast of problems as they develop. Indicators like the oil becoming murky quickly are tell-tale signs of engine issues. If the oil dissipates faster than usual there may be the generator may have leaking gaskets. Numerous other indicators will give you clues to what the issues are on your machine as they develop. All of the issues can be taken care of at an engine shop.

Chapter 5

Amp Hours

A seamless RVing experience depends on your ability to identify, analyze, and plan for your electrical needs. Additionally, it is defined by your capacity to store electricity and replenish your supply. The aforementioned capability depends heavily on your batteries and their resilience.

What Are Amp-Hours?

Amp-hours refer to a battery's capacity. It is the amount of time for which it will retain its power while a device drawing a specific amount of current is attached.

If a battery has the capacity of one amp-hour, and the device connected to it is a one-amp device, the battery will give power to this device for one hour. To figure out what the battery's depletion rate is, you would convert the aforementioned hour into minutes and then divide it by 10. The answer is six, so this means that for every six minutes the process goes on, the battery spends 10% of its life.

If the battery's sticker says "151 Ah at a 50 hr rate," you will divide the depicted amp hours by the hour rate, which, in this case, will give you 3.02 amps per hour for a 20-hour streak.

The calculations and the resulting answers should be treated as approximations as many environmental factors will affect the performance of the battery. Examples include, ambient temperature, power leaks along the circuit, and the battery type among many others.

Note that the higher your energy demands on a battery, the quicker its power dissipates, meaning you will get fewer amp-hours out of it.

Calculating Your Needs

The first rule of using a battery is to never let them drain completely. Different battery chemistries allow for different depths of discharge (DoDs). The average deep-cycle battery, for example, has a DoD of 50%. Every time its capacity drops below 50%, its life span shortens as well as its capacity to hold energy, and this will be a major factor in your calculations.

The average deep-cycle battery has 105 Ah. The first thing you will do is multiply the Ahs by the number of coach batteries you have connected, this is assuming that all the batteries are the same. If you have four, it will give you 420 Ah. The next step is to divide this number by two (because you will only be using 50% of each battery's life). The resulting amp-hours will be 210Ah.

Next, you will need to ascertain the total power you will require from these batteries per hour on average. You will factor in measures that you will take to keep the demand as low as possible and you will take these measures because the battery"'s capacity drops at a rate that is proportional to the size of the demand on it. The aforementioned total will be in watts and will include what is required by the inverter (in watts).

To get a reading that is as accurate as possible, you will need to ensure that you add up the wattage of all the appliances in your RV. From there onwards, figure out what will be used simultaneously and then calculate your highest possible requirements and add some for spare.

Device	Watts	Duration of Operation (hrs)	Watt-Hours	Voltage	Amp-Hours
Fridge	500	24	12,000	12.7	944.9
Furnace	1,000	1	100	12.7	7.9

Micro-wave	800	0.35	280	12.7	22.0
Coffee Machine	700	1	700	12.7	55.1
Total	3,000	26.35	13,080	12.7	1,089.9

Relionbattery.com, 2020.

The table above depicts an example of what your daily electronic requirements may be. Note the total amount of amp-hours required per day is 1,089.9. That is an exorbitant amount and thus you will need to make a few changes. A logical place to start would be the fridge. Consider cutting its running hours and perhaps swapping it out with another energy source.

Device	Watts	Duration of Operation (hrs)	Watt-Hours	Voltage	Amp-Hours
Fridge	500	12	6,000	12.7	472.4
Total	3,000	14.35	7,080	12.7	502.3

With the running time of the fridge reduced by 50% and assuming that you arrive onsite with your batteries at capacity, you will only need to recharge twice a day. If you intend on being away from resupply opportunities for an extended period, perhaps you can cut out electricity for the fridge altogether. Since you will want to save generator fuel (by recharging less), a solar kit becomes essential.

Device	Watts	Duration of Operation (hrs)	Watt-Hours	Voltage	Amp-Hours
Fridge	500	0	0	12.7	0.0
Furnace	1,000	1	100	12.7	7.9
Microwave	800	0.35	280	12.7	22.0
Coffee Machine	700	1	700	12.7	55.1
Total	3,000	2.35	1,080	12.7	85.0

In the table above, it becomes quite apparent that there needs to be an alternative for a power-guzzling fridge. A good solution here would be to run it off the alternator during drive days, solar power during sunny days, and, because propane is not very effective for fridges, it will suffice for overcast days when cooling is less of a challenge.

Building Your System Around Your Needs

This is the point where you decide what is important for you. What are your hobbies, passions, and habits? What is so important to you that you have to bring it with you on your boondocking expedition?

If it is football, then the TV goes along with a signal booster. If it is beer, then perhaps the fridge will have to run on electricity after all. If you like baking, the furnace will be a priority. All of the above will define electrical supply.

Irrespective of what you enjoy doing from your RV, there is one quality that comes with RVing and that is the convenience of electricity. The more efficient your system, the easier it will be to operate. The more power you have at your disposal, the more you can do with your electricity only.

However, it is not as simple as just adding more batteries as they can get expensive. Also, more batteries would mean longer charging times and certain structural upgrades. One of the benefits of going off the grid is that you can choose your energy sources. Thus there is no longer a need to be dependent on electricity.

A lot of thought has gone into the efficiency of RV appliances. Not having the electrical supply to run all the appliances simply means that you need to make energy substitutions in some areas and compromises in others.

Looking at the aforementioned fridge example, a fridge is a necessity when going boondocking. It plays a key role in allowing you to be independent and self-sufficient. Without it, you will not be able to spend as long in the sticks because your capacity to preserve food will be limited.

So while the proverbial refrigerator guzzles way too much electricity, it is crucial to your experience. What do you do? The solution is to change your fuel source.

This appliance, irrespective of its make or model, will always have its place in the RV. The solution to the energy crisis it may create comes in the form of a multi-faceted and rather flexible three way fridge. It gets its name from its ability to use AC, DC, and propane.

The DC power to the fridge does not necessarily come from the battery. The alternator under the hood will suffice. The AC power to the fridge does not necessarily come from the inverter, as you can use the shore power for AC to the fridge. Propane cooling in refrigerators is not as effective as electrical current and will probably lose the battle on a hot day. Thankfully, solar power blooms as an energy source during summer days. The hotter the weather gets, the better solar power works.

The only time you will ever need to use the propane feature of your refrigerator is when there is no sun, so this will be at night when it is cooler and on those cloudy days. This strategy may seem complicated, but once you understand how your system works, it will make sense.

The other power guzzler is the air conditioner. The average RV air conditioner will devour 450 Ah per day, this means you would have to take on up to eight more batteries. It does not end there because to sustain these batteries, you will need to spend more fuel on your generator. The alternative is to insulate your RV walls and put shades and awnings across your windows.

What many RVers do is avoid using the fridge when not plugged into shore power. Do not forget that your fridge is already taking up some of the AC. This means that you cannot use much more in your RV.

For purposes of temperature control while out in the sticks, rearrange your generator charging schedule to the hottest time of the day. This will allow you to run the air conditioner, too. Do not run the generator just because you need cold air. This is especially unwise if you will be spending a long stint away from civilization.

Another option is upgrading to an energy-efficient model of an air conditioner.

By keeping up the fridge's maintenance, you will ensure that it operates as it should. Cleaning is a big part of maintenance. Dirt hampers the air conditioner's ability to function properly, which results in it drawing more current.

Allowing for More Than You Need

So, if you have four batteries, a solar panel, the alternator charging option for the batteries, and propane as a power source to the refrigerator, you may find that you have a larger amount of amp-hours than you need. However, this overage is never in danger of going to waste. By using less (despite what you have at your disposal), you will automatically need to charge less, as such you will prolong your battery life. With the alternator and solar array present, you will always have charging options for the batteries, and a means to run the refrigerator. These options also serve to cut down on the need for generator running time, and because of this, you will save fuel and make less of an impact on the environment.

Chapter 6

Transfer Switches

An RV can draw on more than one electrical source, AC and DC, at the same time. Incoming AC on an RV is a lot stronger than DC.

With the help of charge controllers, the RV batteries can accept a charge from more than one source at a time. In the instance of a long-drive day, a solar panel hooked up to the battery with the correct electrical management system (EMS) can deliver current in tandem with the alternator. When the battery is fully charged, the EMS will stop both devices from charging.

It is not as simple with AC. As opposed to the DC's 12 volts, AC has 120 volts for a 30-amp RV and 240 volts for the 50-amp RV. Drawing power from both a generator and shore power simultaneously would be catastrophic. Every RV owner knows not to do this, but it is human nature to forget, and thus the creation of the transfer switch.

What Is the Function of a Transfer Switch?

A transfer switch is a three-way circuit controller with two inlets and one outlet. They are used in domestic, industrial, and commercial settings where a backup source of AC power is employed. The three-way switch ensures that an electrical system is not exposed to the grid's current and that of an alternate source at the same time. When the operation of the transfer switch is automatic, this device is more than just a switch. It is a device with complex circuitry capable of monitoring incoming currents. When the voltage of one current source drops below a usable amount, the automatic transfer switch will change to a more appropriate source.

Earlier model RVs had a cable connected to the AC distribution board within the RV that served first as the shore power cable and second as the generator connection. It fulfilled the same purpose as a transfer switch but was more analog in nature.

The next phase of the aforementioned technology is the manual transfer switch. This variant is more of an electrical box than a conventional switch. On that box would be a lever or a dial.

If you added a secondary source of live power while the primary source was selected, the secondary electrical uplink would have no effect. Once you turn the transfer switch from the primary source to the secondary, then the latter is the only source that would work. By toggling the switch, the primary will remain live until disconnected.

The latest version of this switch is the automatic transfer switch. This new switch is especially functional if the generator is hardwired into an RV's electrical system. If you are hooked up to shore power and you start your generator, the ATS will detect the generator current and, as a result, disconnect the shore power and allow the generator to deliver AC to the RV.

The key characteristic of the transfer switch is that it only permits power from a single source.

On the input side of the transfer switch, there are two cables: the generator cable and the shore cable. On the outlet side, there is one, and it connects to the distribution board. The RV's ATS is normally positioned proximal to the breaker panel, intercepting the incoming shore power and generator cables.

The average ATS has a delay mechanism. It waits for a few seconds after it detects power from the generator. The reason for this is so that the generator is properly warmed up and producing enough power before it (the ATS) switches over (rvtechmag.com, n.d.).

Connecting the Transfer Switch

When installing the transfer switch, remember that you are working with AC power. It is the 800-pound gorilla of electricity and can be fatally unfriendly if rubbed the wrong way. If you are not confident in your ability to complete or initiate any task involving AC, leave it to a professional.

Before you start screwing wires down and connecting them, make sure that you understand what is going on. Read the manual, study the innards of your ATS, and draw a diagram of your AC inlets leading up to the distribution board. By sketching it out, you will create a clear picture inside your mind of what needs to be done.

Disconnect all power sources live or dead. Your generator should be off and the shore power must be unplugged. If you have an inverter, disconnect this, too.

Read the installation manual and double-check the colors of your wires. Pay specific attention to which terminals they are matched to.

Make sure you have the correct tools for the job. These normally include screwdrivers and wrenches among other things.

The Function of a Second ATS

As you now know, inverters produce AC. If you are aiming for full efficiency, you are probably going to need an inverter, and so this would require a second ATS.

An additional transfer switch can further automate the process. It may sit on the outlet (which will act as an inlet to this secondary ATS) from the first ATS and the cable from the inverter. On this switch, it will be best to set the priority to the outlet of the first ATS as it controls the more robust sources of AC (generator and grid). This solution, while practical, can become confusing to even the best of minds.

Hybrid inverters make it simpler for RV systems that have three AC sources. The hybrid inverter unit is capable of converting AC to DC and doing the reverse. When it detects incoming AC, the hybrid works as a converter and charges the coach batteries. When the AC from the generator or grid ceases to flow, the hybrid functions as an inverter. When this happens, the directional flow of the current is reversed and DC flows from the battery through the inverter and comes out on the other side as AC, which then feeds through the distributor board.

Simplified, the power from the first ATS (the only ATS necessary when using a hybrid inverter) flows through the hybrid inverter to charge the batteries. When the hybrid inverter senses that the AC entering it has stopped (because neither the generator nor the grid is supplying), it registers that the RV no longer has an AC source. The hybrid unit switches functions to replace the missing AC. It works as an inverter would, drawing power from the batteries and converting it to AC. This AC would then flow into the distributor board and feed the necessary appliances.

Chapter 7

Batteries

The battery is the life nucleus of RV dry camping. Every RV needs two battery systems. The system that kick-starts a vehicle's engine to life only needs one battery, but the system powering the living quarters of an RV often consists of at least four. The level of investment that goes into it speaks to the results that you get out. These results include comfort and your level of freedom (how long you can stay off the grid).

Different Types of Battery

Batteries are not all the same. Each model comes with the chemistry that constitutes its capacity for charge, lifespan, and efficiency. Like with all items of material value, a battery's constitution and quality are proportional to its price tag.

Deep-Cycle batteries

These are usually lead-acid batteries with the capability of being deeply discharged. While the best practice entails discharging no more than 50%, these batteries are capable of surrendering 80% of their power. These batteries are different from the usual starter batteries in that they give a sustained current as opposed to a sharp spike that tapers down quickly afterward. Deep-cycle batteries are especially designed to be cycled and can last for up to six years if cared for properly.

Lithium Batteries

These batteries are the latest technology available in DC power storage. An outstanding feature is their capacity to charge quickly. The components of this type of battery are nickel, cobalt, manganese, graphite, and, of course, lithium.

As a testimony to their capabilities, these are exactly the types of batteries that power electrical vehicles. Their capacity to deliver a sustained stream of energy is what makes them perfect for the job. Provided a lithium battery is only discharged to 50% before being recharged, it is capable of lasting for 5,000 cycles over 10years (club4x4.com.au, 2019).

Note that a lithium battery can be discharged, if necessary, to a 20% power low before recharging is needed (Rushworth, 2015).

Absorbent Glass Mat Batteries

The absorbent glass mat (AGM) is the latest sealed lead technology and does not need maintenance. The AGM has a DoD of 80% and is known for its reliability even after being deeply cycled.

Unlike the flooded lead-acid battery, the AGM is less prone to sulfation (sulfur build-up) and can stand for months without attention or maintenance. Like other batteries, it stores best when fully charged because this averts the process of sulfation. Its self-discharge rate is minimal, hence there is a slim likelihood of you needing to rejuvenate it before each use (Buchmann, 2020).

The AGM battery can last for up to three years. By maintaining it well, you can add five years onto it, but this would mean that it is never overcharged (William, 2020). Additionally, it would need to use its specific standard-issue charger only, as other brands tend to cause sulfation.

What makes this battery a good fit for RVing is its heightened immunity to vibration and that it is spill-proof.

The AGM is highly susceptible to overcharging, however, so when installed on an RV the correct EMS is vital. Its higher power capacity makes it costly to manufacture and thus it tends to be relatively hard on the consumer's pocket.

Golf Cart Batteries

The golf cart battery is favored for its resilient reputation. While they are mostly available in six volts, RV owners who use them know to wire them in batches of two (in a series) to make 12-volt units (Leah, 2015).

These batteries are not the same as car batteries in that they are capable of a sustained flow of energy over an extended period of time.

These batteries are available in flooded lead-acid, AGM lead-acid, gel lead-acid, and lithium-ion.

Golf cart batteries have a big DoD threshold and shed up to 80% of their energy reserves but that is the very lowest that they should be allowed to fall. By preventing the golf cart battery array from falling below 60%, you can extend its working life span by up to 50% (Golf Cart Battery Maintenance, n.d.).

The average lifespan of a well-maintained golf cart(acid lead battery) is seven years (Kleinle, n.d.).

Gel Cell Battery

The gel cell lead-acid battery is modulated by an internal valve. The battery consists of a combination of sulphuric acid and silica. When the former and the latter mix, the result is a gel-like substance.

The aforementioned lead-acid quality of this battery prevents fuming and makes it a low-maintenance power unit. Additionally, gel cells do not leak and cannot spill and thus are appropriate for transit over rough terrain.

While still not recommended, you can deep cycle these batteries with minimal damage. The gel is highly sensitive to overcharging so the slightest excess in charging starts a course of irreparable damage. This type of battery is highly susceptible to hot environments, which may contribute to a shortened lifespan (Northeast Battery, 2017).

Lead Acid Battery

This cell is composed of two lead electrodes immersed in a mixture of sulfuric acid and water. The standard lifespan of this kind of battery is between three and five years. In extreme circumstances, given the correct care, it may last up to a decade.

The average lead-acid battery is capable of 100 cycles in its life span. When in storage, this battery needs to be connected to a trickle charger. The device keeps the battery in a usable state by dissolving any sulfur build-ups.

This battery is especially susceptible to self-discharge and for its own health should not be allowed to regress below 70%. The effects of a deep discharge on a lead-acid battery are irreversible.

One of the dangers of this kind of battery is its acid content. Should its integrity be compromised and the contents spill, this is likely to cause damage to all it comes into contact with.

Monitoring Batteries

Every battery bank needs to be monitored. Battery monitors can range from simple to complex but all are designed to give you a better grasp of your power expenditure.

Once your vehicle stops, some systems will need changing over. Your fridge that was running off the alternator needs to go into its propane mode, for example. Forgetting to make the switch could prematurely drain your batteries and you would need to reach for the generator early in the trip. Monitoring systems would help avert this scenario.

Battery monitoring systems keep track of the battery's output or input with displays that are proximal to the battery bank. Top-tier battery monitors are capable of both the former and the latter while having displays that are remote and can be placed inside the RV in a place where they can be easily monitored.

The Shunt

The shunt is a low-resistance conductor that works in tandem with the battery monitor. It is capable of transmitting accurate information to the monitor display. The shunt is normally hooked up to the negative terminal of a battery and gives information regarding the amp-hours, battery life, and amps (bogartengineering.com, n.d.).

Battery monitors along with shunts are integral components of your power planning.

Battery Isolators

The function of a battery isolator is suggested in its name. It serves to compartmentalize the two battery systems in a motorhome. If your DC coach system fails and the battery drains, the power-needy appliances automatically draw from the next available source, which, in this case, is the starter battery. Unless you have a generator or solar to rejuvenate your system again, you will be in serious trouble, especially if you are far from any help.

Solenoid Isolators

The solenoid version of this device closes the circuit when the vehicle's engine is operating, allowing for power to flow from the alternator to the coach part of the RV. When the engine is stopped, the solenoid disconnects the circuit, disallowing any current flow in either direction.

These are automatic, so they are install-and-forget devices that are not very expensive (De Maris & De Maris, 2009).

Solid-State Isolators

The solid-state version of this device acts as a one-way gate between the alternator and the coach battery bank. When the alternator stops running, the current stops flowing. This kind of isolator is prone to voltage loss when the alternator is in operation (De Maris & De Maris, 2009).

Electronic Isolators

This is a unique and recent market entry. Not only does it have a smaller voltage drop rate but it also allows you to charge your chassis battery from your coach array should the former go flat. Additionally, this device is capable of detecting shorts and reacts by depriving the affected area of current (De Maris & De Maris, 2009).

Shorter Cables Work Better

The main reason for keeping cables as short as possible in RVing is to avert attenuation in the flow of electricity. Attenuation is better known as a voltage drop and defines a scenario where the voltage entering a wire is more than the voltage exiting the wire due to the lost energy along the length of the conductor.

Ohm's law better defines this through the formula $V = I \times R$. Simply put, should the current or the resistance increase, so does the voltage drop.

Cable Gauges

One way of averting this is by using thicker cables and only the lengths that are necessary without excessive play.

The width of a cable is measured according to the American width gauge (AWG). As the number attached to this unit descends, the width of the conducting wire's core ascends.

Every device comes with a cable gauge that befits its amp draw.

Low-power lights in a domestic setting and LEDs generally require no more than 10 amps. The wire carrying the current to it is 1.02 millimeters in diameter and classed as 18 AWG. This particular gauge can carry 10 amps but not very far before the voltage starts dropping.

In the case of a 12-volt battery, the lowest gauge you will want to use is 14 AWG. Since this is only effective over a maximum of four feet, a 14 AWG cable is best used between batteries and inverters/converters.

For longer distances, the gauge needs to drop and the width of the cable needs to increase.

For your 120-volt service, you will need a 10-AWG cable that is capable of carrying a current for 64 feet.

One of the consequences of having a cable too narrow is that it heats up and may become a fire hazard.

Chapter 8

Solar Power

Environmental sustainability is high on the agenda. For this reason, when boondocking, everybody considers solar power as an option. Not only is it eco-friendly but it's also cheaper, too. Once the setup is complete, it requires only cleaning and the odd repair. Solar power is the most common alternative energy source for electricity from among others like wind, kerosene, gas, wood, or coal.

Who Needs a Solar Array?

If you are camping out at an RV park, there will very likely be an electrical pedestal that is going to be your first option for replenishing your energy resources. If you are in the city, chances are you will not be spending more than one night there and thus your battery array will suffice.

Suburbia is not the natural habitat of your RV, so unless it's parked at your home or in storage, it can be there only for a brief stopover in exigent circumstances. It is not wise to pack out your full array of capabilities when in the city. Instead, it will be prudent to operate as simply and as minimalistic as possible.

Since a solar array creates DC power, its current is mainly a charging source for the batteries. If you have a class B RV and drive regularly on your boondocking escapades, then the alternator will serve the same purpose just fine. While class A RVs have the same capacity, these vehicles generally park up for long periods with all errands being done in a smaller vehicle that makes the trip, too.

The times when you will not be using your solar array will all be city-orientated. While you are out in the boonies just sitting there and baking in the hot sun, the thought will linger after you have read this: *I should install solar panels.* The thing about solar panels is, no matter how little they contribute in comparison to other sources, they contribute for free. After a week in the sticks, you will start paying attention to dwindling resources like generator fuel. It is at this point that a solar array will prove its worth.

Will you be bouncing from RV park to casino parking and car parking lots? If so, then the True Boondockers Committee-at-Large will tell you that you may be a Wally Docker, Mooch Docker, or Blacktop Docker, but you are not a true boondocker and, no, you do not need to consider power. It just boils down to how hardcore an outdoors person you are.

If you hide out in the middle of nowhere away from society, your inlaws, and the government for a fortnight at a time, then solar panels are worth the consideration. They increase your potential time off the grid.

How Much Solar Power Do You Need?

Solar Panel Watts	Average Sunlight Hours	Multiplier	Total Watt-Hours Per Day
400 x	6 x	0.75	1,800

Vivintsolar.com, n.d.

As with the calculations done for battery power and inverter requirements, the power needs need to be established to define your solar power needs. The initial setup costs of a solar array are costly. This said, you may find that they are well worth the money.

For 450 watts to 500 watts of solar energy, you will need to spend between $2,500 and $3,000. This energy will come in the form of three solar panels capable of feeding your fridge and charging your battery at the same time.

In the table above, the solar panel watts in the first column multiplied by the second is equal to 2,400, which is then multiplied by 0.75 (or divided by 75%) to give you your pool of watt-hours per day, which, in this case, is 1,800 (vivintsolar.com, n.d.).

There will be days when it is cloudy with no or intermittent sunshine, and this will affect the solar array's output. Therefore, it is best to treat the results of your calculations as a guideline to your solar setup's capacity.

What Are the Components of a Solar Setup?

The RV solar system needs numerous components to work. Some of these devices are normally within the pre-existing infrastructure and are easily paired up. Either way, there are one or two specific things that every solar panel needs to work effectively.

Solar Panels

To make it simple, most solar boards come in 100-watt panels. At this rate, you will need about four to make it worth your while. This will not cover all of your electrical needs, but it will alleviate your dependency on other electrical sources, specifically generator fuel.

Controllers

The general rule for controllers is that they are necessary if a panel produces a watt or less for every 25 amps of battery life. The function of the controller is to regulate the amount of energy heading to the batteries. This is an important function that serves to preserve battery life, a function that a hybrid inverter or converter cannot provide.

There are two different types of controllers:

- Maximum power point tracking controllers (MPPT) are converters that convert only photovoltaic (PV) and turbine energy, which is produced in DC. In short, this is a DC-to-DC controller that maximizes the solar array's output without endangering the battery bank. The later

generation charge controller is capable of relatively high performance on sunless days and is favored on bigger rigs. Solar arrays regulated by this kind of controller are wired in a series (solarreviews.com, 2021).
- Pulse width modulation controllers (PWM) tend to reduce the power output to a compatible stream. The arrays that are compatible with this kind of controller need to match the battery bank's voltage and this is limiting. As such, all PWM-regulated solar panels are wired in parallel (morningstarcorp, n.d.).

Batteries

The battery bank is where the power goes. At this late stage of advancement, you should have batteries. The solar power will flow through the controller, then to the inverter (if it is a hybrid inverter) or directly to the batteries. Batteries that work best with a solar array are of lithium chemistry.

Pre-Existing Infrastructure

The existing infrastructure on an RV downstream from the solar controllers is capable of using current contributed by the solar panels after it is absorbed by the batteries. The inverter plays its role by absorbing its share from the batteries and converting it to AC, while the batteries supply the DC demands of a system.

Best Practices

While a great deal of what is needed to complete a solar set up may be inherent in an electrical system, there are ways to optimize the RV electrical system so that it can utilize solar power efficiently.

- **Use Energy Efficient Appliances**

  As mentioned, one way of increasing efficiency is to replace all older items with newer ones. The later the model, the more energy conservative the appliance. The fridge and air conditioner remain high on the priority list.

- **Turn Off All Items That Are Not in Use When Charging**

Be it an inverter, or a laptop charger that is still plugged into a wall socket, they are constantly leaking power off the battery. To see the effects of your solar array, make sure that there is as clear a definition as possible between charging your batteries and using them.

- **Use Lithium Batteries**

It is common knowledge that the initial setup of a solar array is costly, but given the returns on it, many people find it worth the money. Lithium batteries are the new fad because of their ability to absorb a lot of charge over a shorter period of time. These batteries maintain that power for longer, even while being used. These perks are long-standing but come at a higher price, further inflating the costs associated with this energy setup.

- **Choose High-Quality Panels**

Monocrystalline panels consist of single-crystal silicon cells as opposed to their polycrystalline counterparts. The silicon crystal quality makes the former a lot more efficient. Therefore, you will need fewer solar panels, thus allowing for more roof space (energysage.com).

- **Keep the Panels Clean**

Dust and dirt impede the solar panels' ability to absorb the sunlight.

- **Be Wary of Shading**

    If rooftop fans and air-conditioner covers cast the smallest amount of shade on the panels, then this will lead to a substantial loss of current output.

- **Set Up With Accommodations for Tilting**

    When you install your solar panels, make sure that they are permanent and the job is solid, but allow for maneuverability. As the day goes on, the earth turns and thus the angle at which the sun hits the panels differ, changing the rate of UV absorption.

Tilting for Optimal UV Absorption

Since you cannot control the angle of the sun, you will need to angle your panels for optimal performance and thus they should be able to lift and face true south. The logic behind this is that because you are in the Northern Hemisphere, you want the panels to face the equator. The equator is the imaginary line that the sun shines on at a 90° angle.

There are a few different methods as far as tilting is concerned.

Tilting According to Time of Year

Time of Year	Tilt Angle
Winter and Fall	20°
Spring	45°
Summer	60°

In the colder months, the sun is closer to the horizon and thus a steeper angle is necessary for optimum absorption. The recommended setting is 20° (dualsun et al., 2019).

In the spring, the sun is a bit higher and thus the better angle is 45° and in the summer it reaches its highest arc in the Northern

Hemisphere skies, and the angle with optimal results is 60° (dualsun et al., 2019).

The above-mentioned method is a generalized approach to tilting.

There are tilting kits available on the market for anywhere between $75 and $100. These accessories could cumulatively equate to the power generation of an additional solar panel.

Tilting According to Your Latitude

Latitude	x 0.9	+ 29°	Tilt Angle
40°33"	36.3	65.3	65.3°

de Rooij, n.d.

When using this method, the first thing you will have to do is find your latitude. Once this is done, you can do the sums. For this example, the latitude line in question is 40°33" north of the equator. This will put you in line with the Rocky Mountains. The number of this lateral line multiplied by 0.9 will give you 36.3, and then this number is added to 29 to give you your optimum angle of absorption.

This method of tilting is more specific and focuses on getting the most of the sun according to your position on the globe.

With correct know-how, you will start seeing the difference from day one as your generator fuel bill will be lower. With the correct care, your solar panels can last you a decade.

Alternate Energy Sources

While electricity is the dominant energy powering the RV experience, boondockers often rely on alternatives to take the load off the power reserves. The use of fossil fuels to generate heat and fridges' cold air have become quite popular.

It is noteworthy that heat-producing appliances draw more power and, for this reason, it is always more energy efficient to substitute these devices for items that use energy alternatives.

Burning fuels like propane have proven their worth in boondocking. As mentioned, they can lift a big load off the electricity reserves when being used for fridges.

In addition, propane is also effective for cooking and furnaces. Heating water for showers can take a lot out of the batteries and thus propane fills the gap again.

Burning kerosene emits harmful fumes and is thus unhealthy for enclosed environments.

Fire as a cooking method will alleviate dependency on the usual energy sources and can be an adventurous activity. Indoor heating is also possible with the availability of the correct alternate energy source appliances on the market.

Part 3

Optimizing Your RV

Chapter 1

Types of RVs and Their Functions

There is an amazing variety of recreational vehicles on the market today and they are all designed in a manner that is suited to different needs. There is also a large market for used RVs and the price difference between the old and the brand new is vast. The reason for this is that, even though the RV may have been looked after, the price depreciates quickly when in use.

Travel Trailers

These are the most popular recreational vehicles. They allow for a certain degree of maneuverability and mobility when parked and set up for a stay. As opposed to the usual camper van, they have a standalone capacity that allows the boondocker to leave the site without having to break down the camp.

Many confuse travel trailers with camping trailers. In certain aspects, the two are quite alike. The main difference is that the camping trailer offers a more immersive outdoor experience and the travel trailer is designed to protect the user from the elements of the wild.

The travel trailer is sturdy, given its high level of security and optional slide-outs for extra space. The price tag for this kind of RV can be anywhere between $11,000 and $35,000.

Class A Motorhomes

This is the big boy on the scene. The Class A motorhome looks like a bus and, if you really have the money to spare, you will probably buy the one that comes with a slide-out. This is literally the size of a bus and, accordingly, to drive this you would have to be able to drive a bus.

The interior of a Class A RV is spacious and can sleep a small family comfortably.

Boondockers who can afford this kind of motorhome usually buy a trailer and take along a smaller vehicle for added mobility when in camp.

The average Class A RV comes with a 120-volt or 240-volt 50-amp split service. Its generator, which is usually built-in, uses gasoline or diesel and has a direct connection to the fuel tank of the RV.

For the basic models, you can expect to pay in the vicinity of $100,000. Once you get into the luxury league, you will be looking at anywhere between $200,000 and $300,000 depending on the specs (Richardson, 2020).

The Class A motorhome is the top tier of RVing and normally comes with all the bells and whistles.

Class B Motorhomes

Though this RV follows in alphabetical order, it certainly is not the next level of luxury. The Class B motorhome radically contrasts with the decadence of the Class A. Class B vehicles are usually built on a van's chassis, have better fuel economy, and are a lot smaller both on the inside and outside. Thus, these rigs are easier to handle and will house two people comfortably.

The height on these vehicles tends to be just enough to accommodate an average-height adult comfortably. For this version, you can expect to pay between $60,000 and $190,000 per unit (campingfunzone.com, 2019).

These RVs are available in a variety of different brands and are often the result of aftermarket conversions on van bodies.

Class C Motorhomes

The Class C motorhome seems to bridge the vast gap between Class A and Class B. In comparison with the previous two, it is of medium size. Its box is attached to a medium-sized truck or bus chassis. It is easily discernible with its over-cab bulge that serves as a sleeping area. The Class C motorhomes' interiors lean in the way of luxury rather than economy.

It has more space than the Class B RV and can carry up to six people and thus is a little bit heavier on gas than its more economical cousin. You may find that the diesel version of this class of RV is quite common. Class C RVs are available in front-wheel or four-wheel drive and are fitted with larger wheels than the Class B Motorhome.

Another salient feature of the Class C RV is its capability to tow an OHV or a small road vehicle (campingmaniacs.com, n.d.).

Class C RV prices range between $50,000 to $100,000, with the price climbing as high as $250,000 once you start looking at late releases and luxury (Scarpignato, 2018).

Fifth-Wheel Trailers

Being a type of trailer, this RV gets its name from the type of coupling it uses to hook onto the truck. The fifth-wheel trailer boasts more interior space and, because it is a separate unit, it allows for more maneuverability.

As per industry standard, it is 8.5 feet wide at the most, and a maximum of 45 feet long. These RVs can weigh up to 13,000 pounds, hence you need the appropriately sized truck to tow it. Due to the trailer's proportions, the campsites you can access with them are limited (pplmotorhomes.com, n.d.).

The average fifth wheel will set you back between $35,000 and $50,000 and, while this may seem relatively cheap, do not forget to factor in the price and running costs of the vehicle you will be towing it with (pplmotorhomes.com, n.d.).

Folding Tent Trailer RV

If you are looking for economy, then the folding tent trailer is the way to go. As the name suggests, this RV is a combination of tent and trailer and is available in different sizes and configurations. Its design is a lot more frugal and it does not have the electrical sophistication of its bigger relatives. The canvas component of this RV makes it more susceptible to extreme temperature and weather elements.

You can expect the price tag on this kind of RV to be in the range of $10,000 and $25,000. For that price, you would need to pick your seasons and locations carefully. Your time out in the wilderness is likely to be shorter than if you were to use a solid wall RV (lemonbin.com, 2020).

Sports Utility RV Trailer (SURV)

Are you looking for a way to take your dirt bike or scrambler RVing with you? If the answer is yes, then the sport-utility RV trailer is just the thing for you. When Your RV is a trailer, towing an additional vehicle is out of the question. Fortunately, RV builders foresaw this predicament and invented a trailer with living space and storage for a bike or ATV. You can think of this as a mobile home with a garage attached. These are mainly available as modified fifth-wheel trailers and referred to as toy haulers.

The garage function has recently been implemented on Class A motorhomes making them SURV motorhomes.

SURVs can be surprisingly cheap in trailer form, ranging from $11,000 to $170,000. On the other hand, it may bump up the price phenomenally when occurring as a feature in a Class A motorhome. The length of these vehicles vary according to make and the model (19 feet–39 feet) (Sport Utility RV, n.d.).

The Ice Fish House

Do you like ice fishing? Have you ever wished there was a warmer way of going about it? Unbeknownst to some, there are ways to make the experience more comfortable. It is called an ice fishing trailer and people are even building them for themselves. They can range from six feet to 30 feet in length.

The original versions of these temporary accommodations were ice shacks that were placed on the ice of frozen lakes and dams. Today, these vehicles are towed onto the ice, their suspensions dropped so that they sit flush, and fishing lines are cast through holes in the floors of these RVs (Buchanan, 2020).

As you may imagine, these structures are relatively heavy and can only be used if the ice is eight inches thick or more. Any less and the RV may fall through the ice. The average ice fishing rig weighs between 2,000 and 5,500 pounds. As you might know by now, this sport is best practiced in winter. Most ice fishing RVs can second as a normal boondocking RV, too.

You can expect to pay $14,000 for a new ice fishing trailer.

Teardrop Trailers

The teardrop trailer is an RV version of the two-man tent. It is cozy and minimally equipped with electricity. The main function of this vehicle is to provide a sheltered sleeping space.

Due to their size, teardrop campers tend to be lighter. Thus they are easier to tow with more flexibility, allowing the owner access to places that would impede bigger rigs.

Their sizes do vary, and some are even capable of sleeping four people. Other configurations have an opening back section that has space for storage and a basic cooking area. These little vehicles may have the capacity to contain a propane canister, a solar panel, and one or two basic facets of electricity.

For a small teardrop RV, you would pay between $5,000 and $10,000. The going price for a medium-sized variant will be in the range of $10,000 and $15,000. Top of the line, larger versions of the teardrop RV can cost approximately $20,000 (Scarpignato, 2020).

Truck Campers

If your traveling group consists of you, your significant other, and at the most a small child, then this might suffice. The truck camper (TC) is just a box that is suspended onto the bed of a pickup. Space and electrical amenities may be limited.

What the TC lacks in comforts, it makes up for in agility. Due to its pickup base, it can also be a 4 x 4, which gives you an advantage over people with motorhomes and trailers. The boxes for these TC are often sold as an aftermarket product and can be taken off and stored when not in use or left at the campsite when exploring.

The price tag on one of these will be relatively low, ranging from $10,000 to $40,000 per unit not including the vehicle base (Roman, 2021).

Retro Trailer

The retro trailer is a brand-new trailer especially designed according to an old-school theme. These vehicles are often custom-built according to taste and are relatively lightweight.

There may be some on the market that are the real deal (refurbished old-school RVs) and these will sell for a relatively cheaper price. The one way to tell the difference between the refurbished and those built from scratch is by taking a peek at the interior. That will tell all.

The cost of such an item is between $8,000 and $15,000 (Storgaard, 2018).

Chapter 2

Accessories

There are things that you can take with you to make your boondocking experience interactive. Some of these accessories will make your life out in the boonies convenient, while others may require that you use your hands and your mind to make them work.

The Swedish Torch

Some items require you to take a hands-on approach, and this is one such example. The Swedish torch, in its true form, is not something you can buy. For aesthetic purposes, you build it yourself.

It is a simple process that requires a log, spade drill bits, a wood chisel, and a mallet. The log, when standing in an upright position, should be wide enough to balance a kettle on it with some space to spare. You would then drive a hole down the center that extends until about halfway down. You will need to carve out a breathing hole on the side that intersects the center shaft. Done successfully, the log will remain intact upon completion.

The next step is to drive three nails into the log in a triangle around the opening of the vertical shaft. These nails need to stick out at least an inch above the log and vertical shaft and be the same height.

When you get to camp, you will pour some kerosene down the center and drop a match in it. Once there is a steady flame, you can place a pot or saucepan on it, and you will have a continuous hot water source for hours. This is effective for keeping a fire contained and safe during windy spells. It is a good substitute for a campfire, and the wood normally burns out completely, entertaining those watching it late into the night.

Should you be unable to burn the torch out in one go, douse it with dirt, rinse it off, and let it dry. If it cannot be used as a stove again, add it to your next fire heap.

Cell Phone Signal Booster

Remember that when out for an extended period, you will need to adhere to your safety regimen. Key aspects consist of checking in with somebody back home, getting weather reports, and doing research on the next phase of your journey. Due to weak cell phone signals, this is not always possible.

Boondocking in California, for example, normally means heading out of network range. It is for this reason that it is sometimes almost impossible to make contact with the outside world.

The cell phone network booster capable of remedying this is a simple accessory that strengthens your device's signal.

For the device to work, there needs to be at least some network in the area as this device does not generate frequencies, but rather amplifies them. You would also need antennas both inside and outside your RV. A decent brand will set you back by about $1,000 (waveform.com, 2020).

A Reverse Camera

A reverse camera is more of a need than a luxury on the back of a big RV, and this is irrespective of how good a driver you are. These items will be sold with a dashboard-mounted screen along with a wireless camera that you mount high up on the rear of your RV. Not only is this good for backing up but it also helps you monitor the behavior of the drivers behind you when on the road and perhaps your cooking fire while you are inside the rig preparing ingredients.

Most releases have infrared options for those after-dark arrivals and boast a wide scope of vision giving you a clear indication of your back area. Some models are so advanced that they can sense when you are moving backward and thus switch on automatically (tadibrothers.com, 2017).

These will cost you anywhere between $80 and $230.

Fridge Bars

Fridge bars prevent bottles and canisters from falling out when you open the cooler door. This is particularly common after driving over rugged terrain to get to your campsite. These are not only limited to fridges but can also be used in cupboards. These items are either spring-loaded or screw-out mechanisms that jam between the sides of the storage space while clamping bottles and containers against the rear wall.

Improvisations of these are used in bathrooms as towel rails fastened against the wall in the vicinity of the basin. Shampoo shower gel and other bottled cosmetics are jammed into the space between the rail and the back surface.

Depending on the spatial constrictions, screw-out shower curtain rails may get the job done.

Portable Blackwater Holding Tank

The blackwater tank can be anywhere between 20 to 80 gallons. Normally, the size of the RV will dictate the size of the wastewater tank. These tanks are one of the key limiting factors on your stay out in the boonies. Should you want to stay a bit longer, this is what will drive you back to civilization prematurely.

The solution comes in the form of rather flat-looking 32-gallon tanks that will help you extend your visit. These items are sold with pipes and fittings and operating them need not be a messy job. If you still do not like the option, then maybe you should use Doug (the shovel) a lot more.

The truth is the average RV tank lasts for only five days. A backup RV wastewater tank will add another five to that at the most. To maximize their potential, you would need to recycle graywater and use it to flush the toilet. Water-related practices in the RV will need to be trimmed phenomenally.

The prices of these backup wastewater tanks will vary according to the different sizes available on the market.

Cast-Iron Cookware

There is nothing that cooks like cast iron. These pots make the best slow-cooked stews when used on gas or electrical tops, but you will appreciate the true value of these pots when you use them over the fire.

The cast-iron Dutch Oven, for example, can be used for more than just baking. Its lid, which is normally the cover of your oven, can second as a sauce pan.

Aside from the Dutch Oven, there is the three-legged pot that does not need to be suspended. Its three legs make it ideal for positioning among the coals.

Two-Way Radios

The two way radio is especially useful if there is more than one of you going on a boondocking trip. They are handy to stay in contact when you break ranks with your travel partner.

A quality radio is capable of communication over a distance of at least 35 miles and some have built-in weather channels from the National Oceanic and Atmospheric Administration (NOAA). With one of these, you can get a head start on any tornado that may be brewing along your route.

Two-way radios are available as water-resistant, rechargeable, and long range. They are manufactured in different sizes with those employed for commercial use being larger and heavy duty. Two-way radios used in a non-industrial setting will be smaller, more sophisticated and, at the same time, user-friendly. These communication devices are sold with a charging pedestal that plugs into an AC outlet or uses a cigarette lighter charger.

A price for a set of midrange two-way radios will be in the vicinity of $100 per set.

Water Purifiers

Since the water you take along with you on your journey is limited, you will always be on the lookout for opportunities to replenish your supply. Some sources will be natural and others will be from the grid. As you might have discovered, just because water is from the grid, it does not necessarily mean that it is the cleanest. Sometimes, water coming from natural mountain sources will be cleaner still. The quality of water is different at every level.

To be sure, there is a wide variety of filters, chemicals, and mechanical devices available on the market. Some of them work as attachments to RV faucets and others are containers that need to stand for long periods.

- Exterior Filters

    These will normally intercept your drink water uplink to the shore spigot. The exterior RV water filter is usually cylindrical and screws on (or clips onto) one of the water hose's ends. It works on the basic mechanical filtration principle where all the impurities of a certain size are held back. One such example is the inline filter (Russo, 2021).

- Interior Filters

    Interior filters for an RV are all filters that you may use inside your rig. These can be attached to your kitchen faucet head or the pipe and then connected to the underside of the kitchen sink.

    The standard kitchen filter consists of a multistage system: The first bastion of refinement that the incoming water will encounter is mesh. After the mesh comes a porous combination of carbon and zeolite. The two absorb any acidic components from the water. The faster the water passes through this system, the fewer impurities are absorbed.

- UV Purification

In combination with an external mechanical filter, the ultraviolet (UV) system would be most effective. Its biggest victories are against bacteria that still survive the chlorine in the water.

These systems are not normally sold with a mechanical filtration feature. As a purification method, mechanical filtration depends on electricity to work. As such, UV filters are available in 12-volt and can easily be fed by the DC coach system of an RV.

To operate optimally, a UV light bulb needs to be replaced at least once a year. Unfortunately, this kind of purification system also needs to be on and running all the time so it will draw on the battery constantly. The UV purification system is ineffective against the microscopic pesticide's residues that sometimes occur in water.

The price tag on such a UV system can be anywhere between $60 and $200. It is low maintenance and needs no replacements for a year. For it to render the best results, it needs a mechanical filter to precede it on the incoming water supply.

- Reverse Osmosis

    Reverse osmosis (RO) is the most effective form of water purification. Its original design was for the desalination of seawater for use on naval vessels. It is a concept where water is pressured through different filters, each removing particles that the last let through. It is the most effective filtration system and removes 99% of all undesirable matter, whether it is particles, chemicals, or bacteria.

    RO uses more than five different filters, each performing different stages of the filtration process. RO is effective against mercury, calcium, lead, iron, and asbestos. Unfortunately while effective against most pesticides, there are still those that get through. Organic chemicals like radon are prone to beat the reverse osmosis process.

RV reverse osmosis systems are complex and expensive but guarantee safer water. For this reason, it is best to confine this initiative to your drinking water only. The price for this setup will be $350 to $500 (Mortons on the Move, 2021).

Chapter 3

Water, Waste Management, and Temperature Control

Water management is a rather crucial part of your experience. Used incorrectly, your water will be limited and run out prematurely. There is also the consideration of how much space you have to accommodate wastewater.

Water Management

The total water capacity on an RV is normally depicted in a set of three numbers: 60–35–20. The first number indicates the capacity of the freshwater storage tank, the second the size of the graywater tank, and the third that of the blackwater tank. The combination of blackwater and graywater tanks cannot necessarily contain the total contents of the freshwater tank, meaning that the combination of the two may work out to be too small to hold the total amount of freshwater once it has been used.

Storage Methods and Capabilities

RVs hold anywhere between 75 to 380 liters (20 to 100 gallons) of clean water. More specifically, Class A RVs can store up to 380 liters (100) of clean water. The fifth-wheel trailer will comfortably hold 300 liters (80). Class B RVs can carry between 75 and 150 liters (20 to 40), while Class C RVs and smaller trailers are capable of between 130 and 230 liters (34 to 60). Additional tanks and water jugs will boost your water-bearing capacity irrespective of what RV you own (Harmer, n.d.).

Taking Enough Water

The size of a freshwater tank on an RV is proportional to the size of the vehicle in question. The size is, in turn, proportional to the number of people the vehicle can accommodate. The water supply in the freshwater tank will also determine how long you can stay away from civilization.

Water Conservation as a Habit

The seasoned boondocker is constantly aware of their water supply and can cut down usage to between five and 12 gallons a day (per couple).

To achieve this level of economy, navy showers will be the order of the day (wet, lather, rinse). Washing dishes once a day and recycling your graywater to flush your toilet among other strict measures will also have to be employed to create an effective water-saving regime.

Natural Water Sources

In a natural setting, the closer you are to the source of a river or a stream, the purer the water will be. Logically, the cleanest water will be in higher altitude areas. Big rivers and fast flowing water is a safer bet than standing water. Still and slow-moving water is prone to stagnancy especially when occurring in hot weather.

Before using a natural water source, make sure you know what is upstream of it. Avoid natural water sources with commercial farms and agriculture nearby, these are prone to have fertilizers and pesticides washing into the water.

Provided that there are no chemical pollutants in the water you will be able to use it for cooking or washing up. Water from fast-flowing rivers can be boiled and then used for drinking purposes. Bear in mind that, while the limit on your water may be lifted due to the abundance of a natural source, you still have restricted wastewater storage space because you are not going to empty your wash water into this lake, dam, or river, or even on the ground.

Another way of purifying water is by using water filters. There are free-standing variants that operate with gravity and are effective against a variety of waterborne illnesses and pollutants. Aside from your built-in, under-sink filter and the exterior inline filters, the aforementioned will be useful when siphoning natural sources for drinking purposes.

Other Water Sources

The most obvious place to fill up water would be at a campground. Some places offer the service of refilling clean water and emptying waste tanks separately. Other opportunities are rest stops, select filling stations, travel centers, and government-run conservations. The towns that service areas that are favored for RVing are also prone to have facilities for RVs. For example, the town of Quartzite in Arizona services the surrounding area which is a well-known favorite for Boondockers. It is for this reason that Quartzite will have at least the basic necessities for servicing an RV.

Buying Drinking Water

This is instrumental in bolstering the RV's water supply and it is a safeguard against contaminants that may find their way into your RV's freshwater tank. Store-bought water is especially important when faucets have no filters attached. It will keep you healthy if your general water supply becomes contaminated from the source or otherwise.

Taking along additional drinking water is always a good idea. There are different jugs for this purpose and some are sold with drinking water. An additional 14 gallons should not be hard to store and will make the world of difference for your expedition.

The Importance of Being Sure of Your Drinking Water

Stomach bugs while out in the sticks are to be avoided at all costs, as a common cause of this is contaminated water. The ailments and complications brought on by water-borne germs range from short-term discomfort to major long-standing medical implications.

Illnesses like non-tuberculosis mycobacteria (NTM) are common and can even occur in water coming from the grid. NTM is an example of an illness that has long-term health complications and leaves scarring on the lung tissue. A typical hot spot for the bacteria is in showerheads but a sustained stream of hot water will kill it.

Legionnaires' Disease and pneumonia are other examples of waterborne parasites that affect humans.

Other common symptoms of drinking contaminated water are diarrhea, nausea, and hot-flashes. In extreme cases, dehydration occurs, resulting in the depletion of electrolytes, which then causes muscle cramping.

Water Treatment

Effective water treatment is heat. By boiling water for 10 minutes, all bacteria in it is killed. Any water that reaches 125°C (257°F) is safe provided there are no dangerous chemicals in it.

It is advisable to sanitize your RVs freshwater tank once a year or when it smells. An easy way to go about this is to add a half cup of bleach for every 120 liters/32 gallons of water. The water-to-bleach ratio will ensure that the bleach is effective enough to kill the bacteria, but not so potent that it would have any side effects after consumption.

Another method of clearing away any resident bacteria in your water tank is by mixing a 1:1 mixture of vinegar and water. The solution should be enough to fill the tank at least halfway. The next step is opening all the faucets while taking your RV for a ride until you get the smell of the vinegar indicating that the bacteria-killing combination has reached the pipes. When this happens close all faucets to trap the water in these supply lines. Take a leisurely drive back to your base and drain the mixture. Be sure to flush out the water lines and tank thoroughly and make all water drain away. If you have time, let it dry out before adding fresh water so that the vinegar smell will evaporate.

Temperature Control

Manipulating the temperature on an RV involves more than just making it hot and cold. The main reason for this is that there are energy limitations on an RV. Thus it becomes more complex and, as an RVer, you will have to seek out ways to optimize the internal temperature control.

Thermostats

The defining feature between an RV thermostat and the domestic version is the 12-volt DC versus the household 24-volt AC. While domestic thermostats have temperature sensors built into them, the sensors on and RV may be distributed into different temperature zones. By being aware of the differences in the operation between house and RV air conditioners, you are effectively better equipped to regulate your RV temperature.

The location of a temperature sensor will affect the accuracy of your thermostat. If a sensor is on a thinly insulated exterior wall, the reading you get may be influenced by external temperatures. For this reason, you may need to compensate for the positioning of the temperature sensors.

Most RVers are partial to analog thermostats, as these are a standard feature on older RVs but still preferred for their simplicity on later models. As simple as they are, their design makes them inherently inaccurate. The benefit of using a digital thermostat is that you can dial in the exact temperature you want and the device will manipulate your temperature to your settings (or at least try).

Digital thermostats, unlike the more basic analog versions, are multifaceted. In certain cases, these are capable of WiFi connectivity and can thus be controlled remotely. Certain models of digital thermostats are capable of detecting and controlling ambient humidity.

If you have multiple heating or cooling systems in your RV, you will need a dual-zone thermostat. This will usually be requisite in Class A motorhomes, fifth-wheel, or travel trailers. The dual-zone thermostat controls the different heaters, fans, and air conditioners that influence the various RV partitions.

Heating

The first step of keeping warm when boondocking in winter is to dress warmly, but this is obvious. Additionally, if you do get daytime sun, you may want to park your RV in a manner that optimizes your rig's exposure to the sun. When the day starts warming up, you can draw aside those thick curtains and let the sunlight in.

When it comes to heating the RV, propane is a definite favorite. It is clean-burning, economical, and safe. Be that as it may, there are alternatives on the market:

- The ceramic space heater is only practical if you are plugged into shore power as it draws a lot of electricity. If you are boondocking, this will drain your resources quickly.
- Wood stoves will be the easiest on your energy resources. There are small RV-friendly versions available capable of burning anything the conventional fireplace can.
- Catalytic propane heaters are the cheapest and most effective heaters to operate. While they do burn propane, they use their fuel source a lot slower. Unlike the conventional propane heater, catalytic ones do not need a flame to work.

There is another aspect to consider when boondocking in winter. This is the underside of your RV. All water pipes are in danger of freezing if the temperature drops below 32°F. For this reason, proper RV skirting should be installed. If you are hooked up to shore power, you can use a laser heater behind the skirting. If not, you can improvise by adding additional insulation outside the skirting. This can be in the form of snow packed up against the skirting. Soil and plywood boards will also add to your insulation efforts.

Air Conditioners

The correct air conditioner for the job is energy efficient while producing the desired results. In the case of a 31-foot rig, you are going to need two air conditioners. However vital in certain parts of the country at hotter times of the year, these units are still power guzzlers.

So you may want to consider replacing your unit with the latest model of the most energy-efficient units you can find. You can expect them to be a bit pricey.

How to Handle Waste Water and General Refuse

There is no built-in water supply or sewer unit in non-self-contained RVs, and all the heat or cold air is controlled from the driver's cab in this vehicle. This requires less maintenance than those RVs that are self-contained. Boondocking in the former is possible but a lot more rudimentary.

As a rule, self-contained RVs should only dispose of their wastewater at designated blackwater and graywater disposal sites. By no means is it okay to drain these tanks anywhere in the wild, in cities, on the outskirts of towns, or into rainwater gutters. The chemicals used to degrade human waste make it harmful to the environment.

Special accommodations should be made for rubbish generated at campsites. If you are overnighting at a designated RV park, then there will be ample space to dispose of trash. If you are boondocking, all trash, dog pooh, food scraps, etc. need to leave with you. While in camp, use your bin liner and a fox- and bear-proof trash can.

Chapter 4

Boondocking; Fallacies, Truths, and Etiquette

With the usual means of recreation and holiday dwindling of late, boondocking culture has seen a substantial amount of growth. With the increase in this trend, campsites become crowded and many locations that were once considered isolated are now frequented. With the growth of the trend, the need to establish facts, fiction, and etiquette becomes necessary.

Boondocking Myths

There is still the kind of ignorance that breeds myth on the topic of boondocking. Some of these are based on deliberation, while others are based on assumptions and are unfounded.

Boondocking as a High-Risk of Wild Animal Attack

When boondocking, you are generally far from regular human traffic, and this makes whatever wild animal life in the area unaccustomed to people. These animals have a natural fear of people and will thus avoid interaction. Be this as it may, leaving food scraps laying will lure out rodents that, in turn, will attract predators like snakes. With the correct refuse management tactics, this scenario can be completely avoided.

Rattlesnakes are more likely to be encountered outside of camp while hiking. For this purpose, a snake kit is handy to have when boondocking. Snake kits are not curative, still serve to slow the spread of toxins throughout the body and increase one's chances of making it to a medical facility that has antivenom.

Urban Camping in an RV Is Boondocking

Two qualities make boondocking what it is:

The first is the ability to operate in a self-sufficient manner independent of the grid. Yes, this can be accomplished in a town, but the second quality that makes boondocking what it is happens when you are away from a built-up area, human influence, and preferably away from any other human habitation. Although a lot of boondocking happens near other RVers, the fact that it is still in an undeveloped and natural area is what defines it as boondocking.

Full-Time RVers Are Poor

Some think that boondockers are generally impoverished and tend to freeload. People who live in their RVs and travel from place to place sometimes have a lifestyle that is hands-on, outdoorsy, and rugged. This style is often reflected by their appearance, but it does not mean that they are poor.

Yes, there are people who are forced by circumstances to move into their mobile homes, but that is a different story altogether.

Some couples own and maintain large and expensive rigs capable of accommodating almost all the privileges of a domestic environment. To add to this, a lot of RVers are skilled professionals and earn money while on the road. While RVers do not all dress like city slickers, it is an unfounded bias to think that they are all poor (boondockersbible.com, n.d.).

Boondockers Are Dirty and Smelly

When a camper has greasy hands and a brow full of perspiration, these are ways to tell that he or she is a boondocker. They have a thirst for adventure with an industrious mindset that is often paired with a large truck. Boondockers know that going into the boonies is not guaranteed to be a holiday, but it is very likely to be an adventure, and thus they pursue the lifestyle even more enthusiastically. So, they are likely to get their hands dirty and break a sweat from time to time.

Every RV comes with a fully functional bathroom and as an adventurous spirited boondocker you are not going to be dirty and smelly (boondockersbible.com, n.d.).

Boondocking Is Not Suited for Children

Whether or not boondocking will suit children depends on the children. Adventurous parents expose their kids to the outdoors from a young age. Some do it in little doses like holidays and others as a perpetual lifestyle, homeschooling them as they go along.

Suburban parents struggle to pry their kids away from their mobiles, as out in the boondocks there is no cellphone signal. Dispersed camping tends to encourage interactions among families. Boondocking is better suited to families than cities or even developed campgrounds because children can be noisy, which often draws complaints from fellow campers.

Children exposed to this lifestyle learn to be self-reliant from a young age, enjoying activities like fishing, hunting, making a fire, and studying the stars.

Boondocking is safer in that it allows you to rear your kids far from the cities' criminals and bad influences.

Boondocking and Pets

The danger of a chihuahua being snatched up by an eagle if he strays too far out of sight is ever-present, so it is advisable to get a dog that will pose more of a challenge. Cats tend to be more wily, but it does not make them immune to becoming a meal on wings.

There are also snakes in the wild, and they are a very real threat to pets. There are antivenom vaccinations for animals on the market. These are said to prolong the effects of a snake bite, and this means that even after administering one of these doses to an affected pet, the pet will still need a vet.

Pets will need constant attention and monitoring while out in nature. GPS trackers and LED collars are especially helpful for this purpose (boondockersbible.com, n.d.).

Boondocking Facts

Not all of the rumors about boondocking are false. Below are factual statements.

People Carry Guns When Boondocking

Americans enjoy the right to be able to protect themselves. Out in the sticks, there are no policemen and the rangers hardly ever patrol BLM-managed lands. As rare as an interaction with an unsavory character may be, the gun-packing RVer would like to know that should a confrontation transpire, they have the means for self-defense.

RVs Are More Likely to Be Broken Into at Campgrounds Than When Boondocking

RV raiders are just not motivated enough to hang around in dispersed camping areas. If things go missing at boondock sites, other campers are likely the culprits. These thefts are crimes of opportunity rather than premeditated theft.

Habitual criminals are more likely to target known RV campsites. In these cases, it often happens that the camp staff is in on it, too. Thus the chances of getting your RV broken into are much more when in camp than when out in the middle of nowhere.

Not All Rvs Are Designed for Off-Road Transit

Fifth-wheel and travel trailers can be worrisome when towed over rugged terrain. Unlike the Class C RVs with bigger wheels, they tend to have smaller tires and seemingly weak axles. Low-clearance vehicles are in danger of having their bottoms scraped and gouged by rocks protruding from the surface of a road. As such, there is always the risk of puncturing the tanks underneath an RV.

Boondocking Can be Stressful

When boondocking, there are many uncontrollable variables. The freak downpour that turns the access road to your campsite into a marsh or the strange rattle coming from the back wheels of your vehicle can keep you up at night. These things are all part of the boondocking adventure.

Is It Possible to Boondock Permanently?

In an emerging era of digital nomads, boondocking is a favored option among professionals who would have otherwise worked from home. Some people live this nomadic life with entire families and do so successfully. The lifestyle is not an easy one, but those who keep at it do so because they enjoy it.

You Need to Have an Acumen for How Technical Things Work

A lot of the time, you will be away from the services rendered by electricians, plumbers, carpenters, and mechanics. By regularly servicing your rig, many breakdowns can be averted, but with that said, there is no accounting for the unforeseen.

Nobody starts with all the knowledge. You will acquire the know-how by being curious, asking questions, and watching when the professionals work. As time goes on, you will get to know the inner workings of your rig and be able to troubleshoot issues yourself and replace parts or devices.

Boondocking Etiquette

Boondocking etiquette is a list of written and unwritten rules suggesting how the individuals should behave when indulging in the lifestyle. The main purpose of these guidelines is to make the practice enjoyable for all parties involved while keeping it sustainable. Here are just some of them:

Clean Up After Yourself

Whether you are wallydocking, moochdocking, or boondocking, make sure that you remain self-contained and, if you make a mess, clean it up and take it with you or dispose of it in a designated disposal area. The way you leave your campsite is a direct representation of you as a boondocker.

Say Thank You

When leaving your camping area, always thank your hosts, whether it be the campsite security at the gate, the Walmart manager, or the rangers. They will appreciate the gratitude. In doing so, you will leave a good impression and they will look out for you next time. If it is allowed, leave them with a gratuity of some kind and they will welcome you back and perhaps even go out of their way to look after you when they see you again.

Stay for One Night Only

When looking to stay overnight in a parking lot or on private property that is not a designated RV venue, keep your stay to a minimum. Avoid overstaying your welcome at all costs and if circumstances require that you do, make prior arrangements.

Meet and Greet

Meet and greet your fellow campers if the opportunity presents itself. Alternatively, you can at least tip your hat or raise your hand in an acknowledgment. Failing to do so will be construed as rude. Should an emergency arise later, you may even need their help. Greet everybody you come into contact with during your stay. Where required, a few words of small talk will not hurt. Being polite does not necessarily mean you are looking to socialize.

Keep Space Between Yourself and Your Neighbors

Parking your rig too close to another boondocker is a sure way to create an uncomfortable experience. The chances of you and the RV owner who has unwittingly become your neighbor enjoying the stay are slim. Remember the goal of boondocking is to get away from other humans.

Bring Your Own Firewood

Defacing the trees around your campsite for firewood should never be seen as an option, and even less so where the rules forbid. The sound of snapping branches carries and might reach a ranger who is in earshot and who will then proceed to investigate the racket. The consequences may be a fine or even eviction.

Stay on the Designated Tracks and Park on Pre-Used or Designated Sites

While you may be of an adventurous spirit, the preservation of nature always takes precedence. Avoid pioneering new routes and camping sites. Most controlled conservations prohibit this kind of behavior explicitly.

Keep the Noise to a Minimum

Children and dogs are generally noisy campmates. If you have them traveling with you, distance yourself from other campers. Boondocking and loud music do not go together and neither is yelling and catcalling appropriate. Enjoy the sounds of nature and keep noise pollution down to a minimum.

Chapter 5

Turning Your RV Into a Workspace

Modern technology makes working remotely more than just possible and many aspects of modern life make it necessary. As such, more and more people are changing their lifestyles to become digital nomads. This emerging way of earning a living creates freedom which opens up a whole new plethora of opportunities.

Working in your RV while traveling alone is not the hardest thing in the world. Should the number of people accompanying you increase so will the fun, but also the amount of distraction, it is here that the challenges start. There is a multitude of factors to consider before taking on this lifestyle. The success of such a venture depends on the preparation thereof.

What many people do not communicate when broadcasting their adventures as digital nomads, is the necessity for finding the balance between enjoying this new lifestyle, and making it work.

Finding the Balance

The ultimate ingredient that will determine your success is organization. If you are new to this scene, you will need to plan your time, journeys, and stop locations. Contingencies are necessary for every itinerary. Every minute of your day will have to go into some kind of preparation for the moments that lie ahead.

In the beginning, it will take a lot of effort, and you will have to make sure you stay organized. As you get familiar with the ropes, working while boondocking will become easier.

The first step would be to figure out how much time a day should go to your work and subtract that from your waking hours.

Note that because your job is your bread and butter, it always gets priority.

The next stage is to establish a basic sleep pattern. Give yourself a minimum of seven hours. You can not fulfill the high-energy demands of your new lifestyle if you do not get your rest.

Be realistic and factor in how much time you will need for chores, cleaning, cooking, and sustaining yourself. Once that is sorted out, whatever time you have left can be dedicated to driving and leisure.

Optimize your drive times by avoiding cities during peak hours. Leave before most people leave, and arrive before they arrive.

The best way, however, is to set aside entire days for working and do the same for driving days and leisure.

The Convenience of a SURV

The garage on a SURV can be seconded as office space, and it will be especially useful if you are a full family embarking on this nomadic lifestyle. The SURV in the form of a Class A motorhome, travel trailer, or fifth wheel will suffice for this purpose.

To run your laptop or PC, reliable power will become a big priority. If you are going to depend on additional electrical appliances such as large screens, lighting, or camera equipment, you may need to customize your setup. If this is the case, your electrical needs and setup will become bigger and more expensive.

Reliable Internet

As mentioned, if you are a digital nomad, this is one area where expenses cannot be spared. Camp WiFi is not to be depended on. If you find an RV park that has reliable WiFi, count yourself lucky. Note that some network administrators throttle your WiFi after you exceed a certain amount.

The best source of WiFi would be your own personal mobile hotspot based on cellular networks. This will be the most reliable of all the options. It is true that not all areas have cellular connectivity, so for the solution to this issue see: Part Three, Chapter 3, Accessories for information on a cellular signal booster.

Create a Suitable Workspace

The same rules that apply to your home office will apply to workspace in an RV. Every modification made should be done with productivity in mind.

• Good Lighting Is Essential

This is an aspect to consider when parking your RV. You may want to avoid overhangs like trees and things that cast shadows throughout the day. Natural light is cheaper and better. Try to pick a spot with a window for your RV office. This will be helpful but also depends on the season and temperature of the region you are in. If you are in a Californian desert environment, you would most likely do the opposite.

• Make Sure That You Have a Comfortable Seat

If you are so inclined, modify your work surface so that it can be seconded as a standing table when necessary. Sitting with your legs crossed in a hunched-over position in your bed is not healthy for your spine. If you do not have a dinette, get an actual office chair. Swivel works better for access but on whether or not you have space for it.

Remember, your work is what ranks highest on your priority list, and for this reason, you will want to invest in it. If you cannot dedicate a specific area to your work, then pack your work items away when you are not using them. That way work accessories and stationery are not lost or damaged.

- **Put Measures in Place to Ensure Your Privacy When Working**

    If you are boondocking alone and there are other campers around, park as far as possible from them. When traveling with a partner, try to telegraph your needs to your significant other in a manner that does not make you single again. The main reason for this is so that you are not distracted.

    If you are traveling with your family, then you may need a way to shut out the distractions. A good set of noise exclusion headphones will do the job. However, when traveling alone, you will want to remain aware of your surroundings at all times. Headphones will handicap your ability to act in a timely way and appropriately should the need arise. Things that may need your attention may come in the form of vagrants or intruders (both animals or humans.

- **Keep Your Work Space Minimal, Clean, and Organized**

    Decorate your workspace by hanging posters and ornaments that make you feel good. Try to keep the workspace as spacious, uncluttered, and well-lit as possible without it being too bright. It is important to have a good source of ventilation, as stale air means less oxygen and will result in you getting tired and then bored prematurely.

Invest in a Quality Laptop

The laptop is the focal point of your lifestyle as a digital nomad. Thus, it should be a device of decent quality. Nothing will upset the apple cart like your source of income breaking down. Pick a device that has lots of RAM and SSD memory because these tend to work faster and allay frustration.

Since the laptop has such an important function, it would be prudent not to use it for anything other than your work. This restriction adds to the longevity of an otherwise fragile device.

A prudent move would be to get an additional keyboard and mouse, along with a laptop stand. These will give your computer a desktop-like quality and make your workspace more comfortable while bolstering your productivity.

Utilize the Front Seat

Converting your front seat into a makeshift office is possible in most motorhomes with adjustable steering wheels. By placing a board on top of the steering wheel (provided that the steering wheel is adjustable), you will create enough space for a working surface. Certain RVs have swivel chairs, and these will make working and access easier. Another bonus of utilizing the driver's seat is that there is no need to pack away your setup until it is your drive day again.

Using a Second RV

When taking to the road semi-permanently, you may find that while you have a travel trailer, one is just not enough. It is not easy to work in the same living space as your family. An alternative would be to convert your pickup into a camper truck and then customize the tow hitch so that you can still tow a camper trailer. As you might imagine, this endeavor will not be light on fuel.

Buying the Correct RV for the Job

The first real consideration is price, and included in the price category are the running costs.

If you will be going solo, then you will not need a lot of space, but a big priority once again will be workspace. With that said, you may want to purchase an RV that can house you and the equivalent of a small work area comfortably.

Chapter 6

Full-Time RVing

This lifestyle has its advantages and can be a lot of fun, but it is not for the faint-hearted. There are some things that you get used to and others that will never grow on you no matter how long you do it. Be that as it may, there are ways to take the edge off.

Adorn and Decorate

Things like framed photos and awards will personalize the space. Attach it properly as opposed to hanging it, as this will prevent it from falling and breaking during drive days.

Plants and flowers add life, while ornaments speak of individual taste. Secure them so that they do not break and then perhaps hang some memorabilia that speaks of your hobbies. A map of North America marking the places you have traveled is a conversation starter for anyone visiting you in your RV.

Make It Smell Nice

Bad smells are airborne in the form of very fine vapors called humidity. By reducing this humidity, you automatically make your environment less favorable for bad odors. As such, digital thermostats with built-in humidistats are better equipped to fulfill this function. If your thermostat cannot control the humidity, a standalone dehumidifier will do the trick.

Trash can be a big contributor to unwanted odors and, for this reason, you will want to store it outside. Try to keep the container airtight and out of harm's way (Spencer, 2019).

While you may want to keep the hot or cold air out, make sure you open your windows from time to time to let that stagnant smell escape before it develops into something ugly.

Once you are rid of the things that cause bad odors, you can introduce air fresheners and diffusers. Note that not all diffuser oils are pet-friendly (Spencer, 2019).

As a natural alternative, herbs like thyme and rosemary work just fine for a room scent.

If you have a bad smell in your refrigerator, a chunk of coal will absorb it over time.

Customize Your Living Space

Initially, you may enjoy the standard look of your interior, but once you realize how many other RVs look the same on the inside, you will consider customizing it. Wear your RV in a bit and then you can add some character of your own.

Extra colors or different furniture will add to the homely feel. If your budget permits, you can reupholster seat covers and redo the painting and wallpaper. LED strip lights are not only fancier but use less energy, and this lighting adds a chic finish to interiors.

Stay Practical

Do not forget your power limitations when working out your running costs before buying that fancy flat screen or blender.

Remember that with RVing, less is more. Avoid accumulating unnecessary memorabilia and, if you have to think about where you are going to put it, you probably do not need it. Every item you buy for your RV is extra weight. Weight means more fuel costs and all items purchased for the RV cost more than their price tag in the long run.

There is a hierarchy of priorities for a digital nomad, and they should start with the workspace at the top. Sleeping accommodations, food storage, and entertainment should all fit in below work in that order.

Maintain Your Bathroom

For a male, this is not the biggest of priorities, as it is easy to take a short walk to mark your territory. When there is a female involved, it becomes a bit more sophisticated and the bathroom moves up on the priority list.

First, it will need to be practical, and this means it needs to work properly. Everything should be done to ensure hygienic and healthy practices. There are toilet chemicals on the market that kill the odor-creating bacteria while breaking down solids. The use of biodegradable toilet paper will ensure there are no blockages and that everything works properly.

Empty and clean your waste tanks at every given opportunity because hauling the blackwater around wherever you go is senseless. When the opportunity presents itself, use public amenities to save yourself the labor. Keep an empty bucket in your shower to collect graywater for extra flushing. Also, make sure that you have hand sanitizer and put a toilet brush next to your toilet.

Keep a dedicated cloth specifically for this area and a formidable detergent for wiping down and cleaning. Do all of this and your bathroom will remain germ-free.

Additionally, colorful shower curtains and fluffy bathroom mats with matching toilet lid covers will make the space more inviting.

Take Along Some Holiday Trimmings

It takes a special and fulfilled human being to be alone for long periods, but there is a limit. If you are on the road alone during Thanksgiving, perhaps you should get onto the beaten track again. Seek out an RV park or campsite where you might meet a kindred nomad and perhaps you will share some festive cheer over a few beers and a Weber grill.

Hang out all the lights and trimmings for whatever the relevant holiday is and try not to feel too nostalgic.

Chapter 7

Boondocking Abroad

America has the best, biggest, and most comprehensive RVing culture in the world. The local industry is far more developed than anywhere else and thus you are likely to have a far better experience domestically.

However, this is not to say that there are not any other countries where RVing is possible. In fact, there are quite a few countries with varyingly RV cultures and adjoining industries.

Canada

The Canadian outdoor culture is similar to that of American one, allowing boondocking at rest stops, Walmarts, private businesses, visitor information centers and truck stops. The backroads of the area you are visiting will offer plentiful opportunities for boondocking. British Columbia is one of the country's most idyllic natural areas.

Much like the U.S., many of the areas have a maximum stay-over period of 14 days.

When considering an out-of-country RVing expedition, Canada should be the first choice as it is closer and thus may work out cheaper. Unlike many other locations in the rest of the world, this country has a very low crime rate, which makes it ideal for a foreign outdoor enthusiast.

Mexico

Our southern neighbors have a few good holiday locations, but safety is the biggest concern in this country. The best way to go about travelling in Mexico would be in numbers with all your valuables stashed out of sight. Adhere to safety measures and do not travel at night (Chris & Lindsay, 2020).

Aside from that, there is a vast variety of attractions ranging from historical to natural. If safety is your biggest concern, then perhaps the bigger cities are to be avoided. Before you enter this country, make sure that you have done your research thoroughly as getting lost in Mexico can be problematic.

Baja is one of Mexico's revered locations for RVing. It is beautiful and safe and there are many private campsites should you be so inclined.

Europe

Europe is the third most densely populated region in the world. For every km², there are 34 people. As such, there is not much in the way of boondocks. Due to the population density, there is a massive impact on nature. There are strict laws prohibiting unnecessary incursions on the environment and prohibitions on wild camping.

While these laws apply to most European countries, the Nordic countries have laws supporting the extreme opposite. Sweden, Iceland, Norway, and Finland allow individuals to camp wherever they see fit. That means also on private farming land just as long as it is 150 meters away from the owner's buildings. A few more surprising exceptions are France, Scotland, Estonia, and Poland, which are known for nonconformist tendencies.

Countries that explicitly discourage any form of camping are Greece, Netherlands Germany, Croatia, Italy, Luxembourg and Austria. (FirstMate_Flo, 2020)

Southern Africa

Southern African has a highly developed tourist industry and, with the exception of Mozambique, the area is relatively stable. The region is teeming with wildlife and almost every single country on the subcontinent has national parks that host all of the fabled Big Five.

The best country for boondocking is Namibia. As a testimony to its name, vast and empty, it is the second-least populated country in the world with just over 2.5 million over an area of

825, 000 km² and 90% reside in the center to the northern half of the country. The southern half of the country is hot, dry, arid, and serenely beautiful with its barren hills and straight dirt roads.

On its Southern border is South Africa, a country of vast diversity in many aspects. It has seven different biomes ranging from the savannas to the unique Succulent Karoo and Nama Karoo, with the rainforest belt on warmer eastern coasts.

While the powerhouse on the continent, this country has a high crime rate. So, while wild camping and boondocking are not advised, there is no shortage of picturesque campsites that are secure. Due to the wildlife attraction in the region, there is a booming outdoor culture, which encompasses the RV rental sector, too.

Australasia

New Zealand is known for its natural beauty. Their version of boondocking is freedom camping and the country is favored by many outdoor enthusiasts t. Like in Southern Africa, the weather is the opposite to the northern hemisphere. The high season, which is summer, is from December to February. Most likely everybody in the Northern Hemisphere who hates winter knows this, too.

As such, the crowds are bigger and the prices adjust to capitalize off the onslaughts. Spring and fall will still have a fair amount of visitors around, but it will not be as busy as the heart of summer. Do note that, while freedom camping is popular in New Zealand, there are rules that prohibit boondocking in certain areas and fines to punish contraventions.

There is an even bigger endemic outdoor culture in neighboring Australia. The country is a lot more open to boondocking and there are numerous sites for camping in the area. Barmah National park offers a forest and river with sun-bleached sands. The wildlife in the area consists of feral horses from a long time ago, emus, and kangaroos. As you will be warned by park officials, be careful when traveling during dusk and dawn as the wildlife tends to be a lot more active during those hours.

Conclusion

Having read through the chapters of this book, you should now have at least a general idea of what boondocking is, what it entails, and how to go about it. You realize that it may be a seasonal event or a lifestyle. You also grasp the fact that there are sacrifices that you will have to make if you partake in this recreation and, most of all, what you should comprehend is that it is not a holiday but an adventure.

The opportunities and the possibilities created by boondocking are not the same as encountered in everyday urban life. Your increased mobility allows you to see more, and with this privilege, you are exposed to different people and subcultures.

There is so much to learn. Every time you are in nature, you are surrounded by millions of species of fauna, flora, geological features, and weather systems that all play a role in your experience.

Every plant and animal has genetic affiliations with species that are far-flung, each belonging to its same genus, order, or phylum.

Behind every star in the night sky, there is a story. Every constellation is a feature in the zodiac and represents something really meaningful in the belief system of some archaic civilization.

The birds you see are distant cousins of the dinosaur, and the rock formation that you stare at from your camping chair were born in an era before humans ever walked the face of the earth.

The roads you drive have weird names, but the stories that they keep alive are what you should seek after. The little-known, one-horse towns are storage vaults full of secrets and folklore that few care to look at or listen to. The monuments and statues are always with a story behind them. They stand and weather the effects of time while trying to keep the legends they represent alive.

"To travel is to learn" (gutenberg.org, 2018). Many do not know of this lifestyle nor the benefits borne of it. The pockets of knowledge that await the open mind and fuel your creative nucleus make you a privileged individual, not because you have the means to do this, but rather because you have the imagination.

Knowing what you do, you are armed to decide as to whether or not boondocking is for you. Your motives for doing it will determine the level of fulfillment you get out of it. Like with any good investment, what you put into the recreation will define your returns. To get the most out of the boondocking lifestyle, it is required that you commit in full. This includes the amount of effort you put into learning, the research, the ideas, and the ingenuity. The money you spend on it is just the vessel. The good stuff is abstract; it is the attitude that you go about boondocking with, and your perspective that ultimately determines experience.

References

AAA Automotive. (n.d.). How Often Should You Change Engine Oil? Www.aaa.com. Retrieved May 21, 2021, from https://www.aaa.com/autorepair/articles/how-often-should-you-change-engine-oil

Airskirts LLC. (2021, January 21). New Inflatable Skirt Product for RV Owners Is a Game Changer in the Camping and RV Market. Www.newswire.com. https://www.newswire.com/news/new-inflatable-skirt-product-for-rv-owners-is-game-changer-in-the-21079671

Ballotpedia.org. (n.d.). Federal Land Policy in Arizona. *Ballotpedia*. Retrieved June 2, 2021, from https://ballotpedia.org/Federal_land_policy_in_Arizona#:~:text=According%20to%20the%20Congressional%20Research

Becker, N., (2006, November 16). Homeowners Clinic. *Popular Mechanics*. https://www.popularmechanics.com/home/how-to/a1053/4202333/#:~:text=The%20typical%20inlet%20water%20pressure

BLM John Day River—Lower Burnt Ranch. (n.d.). Redrovercamping.com. Retrieved June 3, 2021, from https://redrovercamping.com/listing/blm-john-day-river-lower-burnt-ranch/

Blm.gov. (n.d.). Hult Pond | Bureau of Land Management. Www.blm.gov. Retrieved June 3, 2021, from https://www.blm.gov/visit/hult-pond

Bogartengineering.com. (n.d.). Information on Shunts. Bogartengineering.com. http://www.bogartengineering.com/wp-content/uploads/docs/SHUNT%20Info2.pdf

Boondockers Bible. (2019). Vedauwoo, Wyoming, Dispersed Camping Area. Boondockersbible.com.

https://www.boondockersbible.com/camping/vedauwoo-wyoming-dispersed-camping-area/

Boondockersbible.com. (n.d.). Boondocking Myths Debunked. Boondockers Bible. Retrieved June 8, 2021, from https://www.boondockersbible.com/kb/boondocking-myths/

Brady, K., & Brady, O. (n.d.). Kyle & Olivia Brady. Drivinvibin.com. Retrieved June 3, 2021, from https://drivinvibin.com/2020/07/12/free-camping-california/

Buchanan, P. (2020, November 15). There Really Is Such a Thing as an Ice Fishing RV and It's Genius. RV Mods—RV Guides—RV Tips | DoItYourselfRV. https://www.doityourselfrv.com/ice-fishing-rv/

Buchmann, I. (2020, May 7). Absorbent Glass Mat (AGM) Battery Information—Battery University. Batteryuniversity.com. https://batteryuniversity.com/learn/article/absorbent_glass_mat_agm

Campingfunzone.com. (2019, April 21). How Much Does a Class B RV Cost? Campingfunzone.com. https://campingfunzone.com/2019/04/21/advantages-of-class-b-rvs/

Campingmaniacs.com. (n.d.). A Comprehensive Guide To Class C Motorhomes. Campingmaniacs.com. Retrieved June 3, 2021, from https://www.campingmaniacs.com/class-c-motorhomes

Canadian propane Association. (n.d.). Environmental Benefits. Canadian Propane Association. Retrieved May 29, 2021, from https://propane.ca/environmental-benefits/#:~:text=Studies%20have%20found%20that%20propane

Chris &Lindsay. (2020, March 26). Is It Safe to RV in Baja, Mexico? (And other questions you're likely asking).

Calledtowander.com. https://calledtowander.com/is-it-safe-to-rv-in-baja-mexico/

Club4x4.com.au. (2019, December 4). Lithium Batteries—What You Need to Know. CLUB 4X4. https://www.club4x4.com.au/lithium-batteries-what-you-need-to-know/#:~:text=You%20can%20also%20anticipate%2010x

De Maris, R., & De Maris, T. (2009, May 1). Tech Tips—Battery Isolators in Three Flavors. RV LIFE. https://rvlife.com/tech-tips-battery-isolators-in-three-flavors/

De Rooij, D. (n.d.). Solar Panel Angle: How to Calculate Solar Panel Tilt Angle? Sinovoltaics—Zero Risk SolarTM. Retrieved June 1, 2021, from https://sinovoltaics.com/learning-center/system-design/solar-panel-angle-tilt-calculation/

Dictionary.com. (2020, June 12). *English Words That Came From The Philippines*. Dictionary.com. https://www.dictionary.com/e/words-in-english-from-philippines/

Dualsun, Installation, & dualsun.com. (2019, August 22). What is the Optimal Orientation and Tilt Angle for Solar Panels ? DualSun Blog. https://news.dualsun.com/co-en/12/2014/what-is-the-optimal-orientation-and-tilt-angle-for-solar-panels/#:~:text=During%20the%20winter%20in%20the

Energysage.com. (2020, July 15). Monocrystalline vs. Polycrystalline Solar Panels | *EnergySage*. Www.energysage.com. https://www.energysage.com/solar/101/monocrystalline-vs-polycrystalline-solar-panels/#:~:text=The%20main%20difference%20between%20the

FirstMate_Flo. (2020, December 19). Top Destinations for Wild Camping in Europe. Holidaypirates.com.

https://www.holidaypirates.com/travel-magazine/top-destinations-for-wild-camping-in-europe_26090

Freeroam.app. (n.d.). Upper Teton View. Upper Teton View. Retrieved June 3, 2021, from https://freeroam.app/campground/upper-teton-view

Gabrielse, D. (2015, February 11). 10 Quick Tips for Generator Maintenance. Modern Contractor Solutions. https://mcsmag.com/10-quick-tips-generator-maintenance/#:~:text=Cleaning%20the%20engine%20removes%20potentially

Go RVing. (2020, October 5). RV Industry Facts and Figures | Go RVing. www.gorving.com. https://www.gorving.com/newsroom/rv-industry-association-manufacturing-statistics#:~:text=RV%20ownership%20is%20at%20a

Golf Cart Battery Maintenance. (n.d.). Golf Cart Battery Maintenance. Www.golfcartgarage.com. Retrieved May 30, 2021, from https://www.golfcartgarage.com/golf-cart-battery-maintenance/

Gutenberg.org. (2018). Innocents Abroad by Mark Twain, Complete. Gutenberg.org. https://www.gutenberg.org/files/3176/3176-h/3176-h.htm

Hait, A. (2020, September 29). *RVs:* A Way to See America From the Safety of Your Own "Home." The United States Census Bureau. https://www.census.gov/library/stories/2020/09/recreational-vehicle-a-way-to-see-america-from-the-safety-of-your-own-home.html

Harmer, J. (n.d.). How Many Gallons of Water Does an RV Usually Hold? Camperreport.com. Retrieved June 8, 2021, from https://camperreport.com/how-many-gallons-of-water-does-an-rv-usually-hold/?

Https://www.bea.gov/. (2020, November 10). Outdoor Recreation Satellite Account, U.S. and States, 2019 | U.S.

Bureau of Economic Analysis (BEA). Www.bea.gov. https://www.bea.gov/news/2020/outdoor-recreation-satellite-account-us-and-states-2019

Iberdrola. (n.d.). Noise Pollution: How to Reduce the Impact of an Invisible Threat? Iberdrola. Retrieved May 24, 2021, from https://www.iberdrola.com/environment/what-is-noise-pollution-causes-effects-solutions#:~:text=According%20to%20the%20National%20Park

Kampgrounds of America. (2021, April 21). *Fresh Data Indicates Camping Interest To Remain High In 2021*. Prnewswire.com. https://www.prnewswire.com/news-releases/fresh-data-indicates-camping-interest-to-remain-high-in-2021-301273611.html

Kleinle, K. (n.d.). The Life Expectancy of a Golf Cart Battery. GolfLink. Retrieved May 30, 2021, from https://www.golflink.com/facts_4048_life-expectancy-golf-cart-battery.html#:~:text=Lifespan

Lalley, J. S., & Viles, H. A. (2006). Do Vehicle Track Disturbances Affect the Productivity of Soil-Growing Lichens in a Fog Desert? *Functional Ecology, 20*(3), 548–556. https://doi.org/10.1111/j.1365-2435.2006.01111.x

Leah. (2015, April 21). RV Battery: Best RV Deep Cycle Battery for RVs & Travel Trailers. RVshare.com. https://rvshare.com/blog/pick-best-rv-battery-read/#:~:text=The%206%2Dvolt%2C%20golf%20car

Lemonbin.com. (2020, July 2). 13 Types of RVs (Recreational Vehicles) for All Kinds of Vacation Fun. LemonBin Vehicle Guides. https://lemonbin.com/rv-types/

Long, H. (2018, December 28). 1 million Americans live in RVs. Meet the "modern nomads." *Washington Post*. https://www.washingtonpost.com/business/2018/11/12/million-americans-live-rvs-meet-modern-nomads/

Merriam-Webster. (n.d.). Definition of Boondocks. Www.merriam-Webster.com. Retrieved June 9, 2021, from https://www.merriam-webster.com/dictionary/boondocks

Montana, D. (2015, May 3). The Top 10 Questions Before You Choose an RV. RVshare.com. https://rvshare.com/blog/choose_an_rv/

Mordorintelligence.com. (n.d.). Global Recreational Vehicle Market | Growth, Trends, and Forecast (2020-2025). Www.mordorintelligence.com. Retrieved June 2, 2021, from https://www.mordorintelligence.com/industry-reports/recreational-vehicle-market

Morningstarcorp. (n.d.). Solar Charge Controllers | Got Questions? Get the Answers Here. Morningstar Corporation. Retrieved June 1, 2021, from https://www.morningstarcorp.com/solar-charge-controllers

Mortons on the Move. (2021, March 19). Should You Have a Reverse Osmosis System for Your RV? Mortons on the Move. https://mortonsonthemove.com/reverse-osmosis-system-for-rv/

National Park Service. (2021, April 14). Death Valley National Park. Nps.gov. https://www.nps.gov/deva/planyourvisit/backcamp.htm

Nick The Rambling Man. (2020, July 13). Phoenix Free Dispersed Camping Spots. Https://Southwestmicroadventures.com/. https://southwestmicroadventures.com/blog/phoenix-free-dispersed-camping-spots/

Nickels, S. N. (2020). 5 Incredible Free Campsites in Utah (Near National Parks & Attractions!). Eternalarrival.com. https://eternalarrival.com/travel-blog/north-america/usa/best-free-campsites-in-utah/#Best_Free_Camping_Near_Bryce_Canyon_National_Park

Northeast Battery. (2017, September 18). *Battery 101: The Pros And Cons of a Gel Mat Battery - Northeast Battery*. Northeast Battery. https://northeastbattery.com/battery-101-pros-cons-gel-mat-battery/

Outdoorsy.com. (n.d.). *Hult Pond | Outdoorsy*. Www.outdoorsy.com. Retrieved June 3, 2021, from https://www.outdoorsy.com/guide/hult-pond

Ppplmotorhomes.com. (n.d.). Everything to Know About Fifth Wheels | *PPL Motor Homes*. Www.pplmotorhomes.com. Retrieved June 3, 2021, from https://www.pplmotorhomes.com/about-fifth-wheel-trailers#:~:text=Fifth%20wheels%20can%20be%20up

Relionbattery.com. (2020, June 18). How Much Solar Do I Need for My RV? Relionbattery.com. https://relionbattery.com/blog/rv-solar-panel

Richardson, A. (2020, August 15). How Much Does a Class A Motorhome Cost? RVing Know How. https://www.rvingknowhow.com/class-a-motorhome-cost/

Roman, R. (2021, February 13). How Much Do Truck Campers Cost? 17 Awesome Examples Included. Gotraveltrailers.com. https://gotraveltrailers.com/how-much-do-truck-campers-cost/

Rushworth, J. (2015, March 30). Batteries: Lithium-ion vs AGM. *Victron Energy*. https://www.victronenergy.com/blog/2015/03/30/batteries-lithium-ion-vs-agm/

Russo, J. (2021, January 25). Best RV Water Filters and Why You Need Them—We're the Russos. Weretherussos.com. https://weretherussos.com/rv-water-filters/

RVshare. (2021, May 3). Top 5 Boondocking Spots in Oregon | Free Camping in Oregon. RVshare.com. https://rvshare.com/blog/boondocking-in-oregon/

rvtechmag.com. (n.d.). Electrical Tutorial–Chapter 4–Transfer Switches. Www.rvtechmag.com. Retrieved May 31, 2021, from https://www.rvtechmag.com/electrical/chapter4.php

Scarpignato, M. (2018, December 18). How Much Does a Class C RV Cost? RVBlogger. https://rvblogger.com/blog/how-much-does-class-c-rv-cost/#:~:text=The%20costs%20vary%20quite%20a

Scarpignato, M. (2020, March 5). Teardrop Camper Prices: How Much Do They Cost? RVBlogger. https://rvblogger.com/blog/teardrop-camper-prices-how-much-do-they-cost/#:~:text=New%20teardrop%20campers%20can%20range,will%20cost%20%2415%2C000%20or%20more!

solarreviews.com. (2021, May 19). How to Wire Solar Panels in Series vs. Parallel. *Solar Reviews*. https://www.solarreviews.com/blog/do-you-wire-solar-panels-series-or-parallel#:~:text=Maximum%20Power%20Point%20Tracking%20(MPPT

Spencer. (2019, October 19). Six Camping Tips for Keeping Your RV Smelling Fresh. Longviewrv.com. https://www.longviewrv.com/blog/rv-tips-6-camping-tips-for-keeping-your-rv-smelling-fresh/

Sport Utility RV. (n.d.). https://www.travelcamp.com/Travel-Trailers/Sport-Utility-RV-Towable-and-Motorized/. Https://Www.travelcamp.com/. Retrieved June 3, 2021, from https://www.travelcamp.com/Travel-Trailers/Sport-Utility-RV-Towable-and-Motorized/

Storgaard, M. (2018, November 30). How Much Do Vintage RVs Cost? (Helpful Examples). Godownsize.com. https://www.godownsize.com/vintage-rv-cost/#:~:text=A%20vintage%20RV%20has%20an%20average%20cost%20of%20around%20%246%2C000%20to%20%2410%2C000.

Tadibrothers.com. (2017, March 22). How Much Does a Backup Camera Cost? (affordable camera kits). TadiBrothers Blog. https://www.tadibrothers.com/blog/much-backup-camera-cost

Theadventuretravelers.com. (n.d.). Latest RV Industry Statistics, Trends & Data (2021)— Infographics & Charts. *The Adventure Travelers.* Retrieved June 2, 2021, from https://www.theadventuretravelers.com/latest-rv-industry-statistics-trends-data-2021/

Thiel, W. (2021, February 21). Why You Need a Water Pressure Regulator for Your RV. https://blog.campingworld.com/rv-basics/why-you-need-a-water-pressure-regulator-for-your-rv/#:~:text=The%20correct%20water%20pressure%20for,is%20ideal%20for%20many%20RVs.

USDA Forest Service. (n.d.). Uinta-Wasatch-Cache National Forest. Www.fs.usda.gov; www.fs.usda.gov. Retrieved June 2, 2021, from https://www.fs.usda.gov/activity/uwcnf/recreation/camping-cabins

USDA Forest Service. (2021a). Dixie National Forest—Home. Usda.gov. https://www.fs.usda.gov/detailfull/dixie/home/?cid=fswdev3_006645&width=full

USDA Forest Service. (2021b). Dixie National Forest—Home. Usda.gov. https://www.fs.usda.gov/detailfull/dixie/home/?cid=fswdev3_006645&width=full

Utah.com. (2021). Smithsonian Butte Scenic Back Country Byway | Zion National Park.

Utah.com. https://utah.com/campgrounds/smithsonian-butte-zion

Valtzis, S. (n.d.). Sage Hen Hill Road. Www.motogpsroutes.com. Retrieved June 3, 2021, from https://www.motogpsroutes.com/blog/item/6154-sage-hen-hill-road

Vivintsolar.com. (n.d.). How to Calculate Solar Panel Output | Vivint Solar Learning Center. Www.vivintsolar.com. Retrieved May 31, 2021, from https://www.vivintsolar.com/learning-center/how-calculate-solar-panel-output

Waveform.com. (2020). 11 Best Cell Phone Signal Boosters of 2021 [Real-World Tests]. Waveform. https://www.waveform.com/pages/best-cell-phone-signal-boosters

Widmer, B. (2019, April 8). *37+ Key RV Industry Statistics, Trends & Facts (2020 Data)*. Https://Www.thewanderingrv.com/. https://www.thewanderingrv.com/rv-industry-statistics-trends-facts/

William, J. (2020, August 18). How Long Do AGM Batteries Last? *Advance Maintenance tips*. RV Expert. https://rvexpert.net/how-long-do-agm-batteries-last/

www.ingramcontent.com/pod-product-compliance
Lightning Source LLC
Chambersburg PA
CBHW072156100526
44589CB00015B/2245